The Church Polity of the Pilgrims.

A

SERMON,

REV. J. W. WELLMAN,
PASTOR OF THE ELIOT CHURCH, NEWTON, MASSACHUSETTS.

WITH AN APPENDIX.

"Ask for the old paths, where is the good way, and walk therein, and ye shall find rest to your souls." — Jer. 6: 16.

BOSTON:
CONGREGATIONAL BOARD OF PUBLICATION.
CHAUNCEY STREET.

CAMBRIDGE:
ALLEN AND FARNHAM, PRINTERS.

The following Discourse was preached on the 21st of December, 1856, to the author's own congregation, and, at their request, was subsequently published. At the solicitation of the Congregational Board of Publication, it is now committed to their hands. The sermon has been revised, and the notes which have been annexed will, it is hoped, add somewhat to its value. They will, at least, serve to show how numerous and vital are the relations of the subject discussed, and how inadequate any treatment of it must be that is confined to the limits of a single discourse.

J. W. W.

Newton, Mass., Dec. 14, 1857.

SERMON.

Moreover, if thy brother shall trespass against thee, go and tell him his fault between thee and him alone; if he shall hear thee, thou hast gained thy brother. But if he will not hear thee, then take with thee one or two more, that in the mouth of two or three witnesses every word may be established. And if he shall neglect to hear them, tell it unto the church; but if he neglect to hear the church, let him be unto thee as a heathen man and a publican. Verily I say unto you, whatsoever ye shall bind on earth shall be bound in heaven; and whatsoever ye shall loose on earth shall be loosed in heaven. — Matthew 18: 15-18.

On the twenty-first of December, 1620, two hundred and thirty-six years ago, our Pilgrim Fathers landed at Plymouth. The sun was lingering, as he is to-day, about his winter solstice, when they stepped shivering upon the cold and bleak shore. Before them was the illimitable wilderness, full of real and fabulous perils; behind them the vast, uncharted ocean, from whose dangers they had just escaped; and all around, nature, in her midwinter garb, stern and dreary, was frowning upon their approach. But the very feet of those men hallowed the rock which they pressed as they stepped upon the shore, and left it immortal; and to-day it concentrates the veneration and grateful affections of a large and prominent portion of the human race. That rock now is, and ever will be, one of the most conspicuous objects on the broad bosom of the world's history.

That little band of Pilgrims was a fragment of a Congregational church. They had left their pastor and a part of their brethren in Holland, but expected them soon to follow and rejoin them in their exile. They came hither for freedom, — not freedom to do every thing, but to worship God. They came hither to escape ecclesiastical despotism. In breaking away from the formalities and corruptions of the English ecclesiastical establishment, they had gone to the New Testament to learn the primitive mode of organizing and conducting a Christian church. Under that guidance, their church polity had assumed the form of Congregationalism. And it was this external and democratic aspect of their religion, more than all things else, that drew down upon them the wrath of the English hierarchy. Had they been contented to remain quietly in the Established Church, and conform outwardly to all its forms, it would have made little difference what they believed.* But it was just this that they could not do. They had conscientiously adopted another, and, as they believed, the only primitive and scriptural form of Christian worship and church polity; and it was to set up this divine form of a church in the world, and to enjoy it unmolested, that they came to this cold and inhospitable shore. It was for freedom to conduct their worship, and all their ecclesiastical affairs, according to what they believed to be the teachings of the New Testament, — it was for their *Congregationalism* as the most completely divine system of church government, that they braved the perils of the deep, and the greater perils of the wilderness.

Since the year 1769, it has been customary at Plymouth, and at various other places in New Eng-

* "The martyrs of the primitive churches of old lost more of their blood and lives for their meetings and assemblies than for personal profession of the faith; and so also have others done under the Roman apostasy. It is a usual plea among those who engage in the persecution or punishment of such as differ from them, that if they please they may keep their opinions, their consciences; and faith unto themselves, without meetings for communion or public worship; and herein they suppose they deal friendly and gently with them. And this is our present case." — Inquiry concerning Evangelical Churches, by John Owen, p. 256, recent edition.

land and beyond New England, to celebrate the landing of the Pilgrims, on the day of its anniversary, with appropriate ceremonies. But this year it is proposed to inaugurate a new and far more general commemoration of that grand event, namely, a commemoration by all the Congregational churches of our country. This Sabbath is Forefathers' day; and it is proposed that all the churches of our denomination in the land shall have their attention especially directed to the incomparable worth of the church polity of the Pilgrim Fathers. The design is to increase the already greatly revived interest of our churches in Congregationalism as the church polity, not only of the Pilgrims, but also of the Apostles and primitive Christians, and particularly to confirm the justness of its claims to the warm Christian love, and the ample Christian benevolence, of all its adherents. And this is only one of many indications, patent to all, at the present time, that Congregationalism is now asserting itself in our country, particularly in the Western States, as never before. This present movement, therefore, we hail as an omen of great good to living evangelical religion, and to the best interests of our country. It will serve permanently to connect Congregationalism in the minds of men with the exalted character and faith of the Pilgrims. It will greatly extend this primitive church order in this land, and will give it a position and a power such as it has never yet enjoyed. A noble monument this to the memory of that little band of Congregational Pilgrims! — more noble than any ponderous column, though it were of costliest marble, and though it towered to the heavens! For the monument we propose is not material and perishable; it is not the bricks and stones of the temples that may be reared; it is not the robes and the ritual and the sensuous ceremonies of an imposing church establishment; it is not a long and rising grade of church judicatories, as unwieldy and discordant in their working as they are human in their origin and authority; but it is the *truth*, — the towering, radiant *truth of the gospel*, — which shall thus be made to light up the hills and valleys, the forests and prairies, of a continent; it is the living Christian churches, modelled after the simple, primitive form which shall thus be planted among the foundations of a rising empire, working their spirit ineradicably into its historic life, moulding all its popular institutions, and so determining its destiny. It is a monument that will stand long after the bricks and marble of our earthly temples shall have crumbled to dust; long after all gorgeous rituals and imposing church judicatories shall have passed into eternal oblivion; yea, as long as that living church shall stand, which, thus enlarged, shall worship God in the simplicity and purity of heaven's worship, and in a temple not made with hands.

I cannot conceive of any manner of commemorating the landing of the Pilgrims more congenial with their spirit and aims. It is certainly in harmony with the godly zeal of that noble man and pastor, John Robinson, who himself labored most assiduously, first, to indoctrinate all his people in the principles of the primitive church polity, and then to establish them in the practice and love of it; and with so much success, too, that one of our early historical writers, speaking of the manner in which the church at Plymouth conducted their worship and ecclesiastical business before they settled a pastor, says, "The Plymouth people well understood their own principles; .... knew the way of their worship, and were resolved upon it." Would that all their pious descendants who have embraced their system of church government had *known* as much, and had been as fully *resolved to abide* by their principles! Then would the church polity of the Pilgrims have inherited the land. This manner of observing this anniversary certainly accords likewise with the spirit of Brewster and Bradford, and the other leading men of the Plymouth Church, who did so much by mild yet enlightening counsels, that could not be resisted, to induce the first churches in Boston, Salem, and Charlestown to adopt the same church polity with themselves, and who thus actually secured the general and permanent prevalence of Congregationalism in New England. Nothing can be more truly in sympathy with the spirit and aims of those Pilgrim Fathers, than that we to-day put our own hearts and hands vigorously to the work of exalting and perpetuating in our country that same religious faith and order for which they toiled and suffered in the Old World, for which they were exiles in midwinter on a frozen and rocky shore, and which, with such promptness and efficiency, they labored to establish in the subsequent settlements.

Moreover, whenever the attention of our churches is called to the claims of Congregationalism upon their Christian benevolence, the question to be met at the very outset is, What is there in this church polity of the Pilgrims *worth* preserving and diffusing in the world? Would not their creed be just as good if we left out of it their doctrine of the church? Why not accept their faith in every particular except this? Why not give our money to build Presbyterian or Episcopalian or Methodist churches as soon as Congregational? Why not be satisfied with a church if it can only be called evangelical? Why not sustain the various missionary operations and church-extension enterprises of these several denominations as readily as those of our own? Would not this exhibit a more Christian, or at least a more unsectarian, spirit? Is it, indeed, the *Christian* duty of anybody to disseminate and perpetuate Congregationalism? What is there, in other words, peculiarly excellent in our church polity, which gives it a claim, superior to that of any other, to our affection and our benevolence? These questions should be met. The members of *our* churches should "*know their own principles*," that they may judge for themselves whether they are worth maintaining. It is a common complaint among those who have gone from our churches to our Western States, that, while they were in New England, they never heard a single sermon upon their own form of church government.* Consequently, they are entirely unprepared to confront the intense sectarianism which they find so much more vigorously nurtured in other denominations. They do not know enough about their own church polity to understand that one of its greatest excellences is, that it is singularly unsectarian, and that, for this very reason, they should maintain it. They are not aware *why* they have not heard about it. One of its greatest merits has blinded them to its value. As soon as they leave New England they

* See Appendix, Note A.

are met at once with the bold declaration, that "Congregationalism is a very good system of church government for New England; it works well there; but it is a very bad system everywhere else, and it will not do even to try it." And having never been taught that there is any thing of particular value in it, they are not prepared to gainsay such an unadvised statement; and so have quietly fallen in, as if it were a matter of necessity, with some other church organization. And thus it has happened, that, while Congregational New England has done more than all the rest of the country to give the gospel and its institutions to the West, her own church order, until very recently, has made less progress there than that of almost every other evangelical denomination. Now the question is, is this right? Is there, or is there not, any thing *worth* conserving in the church order of the Pilgrims? If there is, upon *whom* does the duty devolve? Bear with me, then, to-day, while I defend, as well as I may, *the faith of the Pilgrims, so far as it respects the doctrine of the church.*

The church polity of the Pilgrims, or Congregationalism, may be commended to our acceptance by a twofold argument: first, by its accordance with the teachings of Scripture; and, secondly, by its pre-eminent fitness to all the ends of a church.

I. In the first place, Congregationalism is scriptural. It was the church polity of the primitive Christians; Christ is its author. He and the inspired apostles taught it, and taught no other church system, either by word or practice. Congregationalism, as a system of church government, may be summarily defined under three heads: first, the nature of the church; secondly, the officers of the church; and, thirdly, the relation of the churches to each other; and each of these parts, and therefore the whole of the system, may be shown to be scriptural.

1. In the first place, a Christian church, as defined by Christ and the apostles, was a Congregational church. The term Congregational was, of course, not then in use; nor would it be now, had it not become necessary to distinguish, by some appropriate term, the primitive form of a Christian church from other forms which have since been invented. What we assert is, that *a church*, according to the teachings of Christ and the apostles, is no other than what we now denominate a Congregational church. The term church is used in the New Testament chiefly in two senses.

It sometimes means the invisible church; that is, all the real followers of Christ, the whole body of true believers. This is the great redeemed company; "the body [of Christ,] the fulness of him that filleth all in all;" his "bride;" the church which he loved and gave himself for, "that he might sanctify and cleanse it with the washing of water by the word; that he might present it to himself a glorious church, not having spot or wrinkle, or any such thing; but that it should be holy and without blemish." In this comprehensive sense of the term, we seem to be warranted in using it to designate either the whole company of the redeemed on earth and in heaven, or the whole company of true Christians on earth. Hence it is very common to make a subdivision, and speak of the church militant and the church triumphant. But it is all, in reality, one body. This is *the church*, and is known only to Him who knoweth the hearts of all men. No human vision can span its breadth and take in its limits. The invisible line of its boundary on earth, running through every Christian community and nearly every Christian family, and everywhere separating the redeemed of the Lord from the world, no human eye can trace; and therefore it is called the *invisible* church.

The second use of the term church, in the New Testament, is when it is used to designate visible, local, organized bodies of professed Christians; as, "the church which was at Jerusalem," "the church at Antioch," "the churches of Galatia." This is the only visible church; unless by a generalization, not according to the practice of the New Testament writers, but to which, nevertheless, there may be no great objection, we call *all* the true churches of Christ in the world the visible church. Nothing is plainer than that the term is never used in the New Testament to designate an organized body of local churches. It never means a collection of churches, any more than the word man in the New Testàment ever means a collection of men, or the word tree a collection of trees. The New Testament writers were not guilty of the absurdity of calling several *churches* a *church.* They never so confounded ideas and abused language as to put together several of *the* churches, and still call the resultant body *the* church. They knew of only the invisible church, and distinct, local, visible churches. They had nothing to correspond to such organizations as the Presbyterian church, the Episcopalian church, the Methodist Episcopal church, the Roman Catholic church, and other centralized systems of ecclesiastical government. When they spoke of a church, they spoke of a distinct, independent, local organization. When they spoke of more than one, they said *churches.* "The *churches* of Asia salute you;" not *the church* of Asia. "So ordain I in all the *churches;*" not in all *the church.* "The care of all the *churches;*" not of all *the church.* When, therefore, we say *the Congregational Church,* meaning the whole body of

Congregational churches, we adopt a mode of expression not warranted in Scripture. For the same reason, the very name, "The Presbyterian Church of the United States of America," shows at once that there is something about that organization that is unscriptural. So of the name of the Episcopalian Church, and of every other organized provincial or national church. We are simply in search after the *truth*, with respect to the scriptural form of ecclesiastical government; and we deny that Christ and the apostles left to Christians any other form of a church than that of distinct, independent, local churches. If they did, doubtless it can be shown.

What, then, is a Christian church, according to the teachings of the New Testament? *It is a company of persons, who are apparently Christians, organized by a covenant with each other and with God, into a society distinct and complete in itself, acknowledging Christ as their only head, and who are thus associated for the purpose of maintaining mutual, brotherly watch and care, and of meeting statedly in one place to maintain public worship and Christian ordinances.* This is the definition of a church as it is described by the writers of the New Testament. It is also the same definition, in substance, which has always been given by the most approved authorities of a Congregational church. A company of such persons thus organized for such a purpose, wherever it is, and whatever its name, is a true church of Christ. Observe the particulars of this definition. The members of a church must be *apparently* true Christians. We do not know that every member of a visible church is what he professes to be; but he must be of such an *apparent* character, that, in the judgment of charity, we can believe him to be a true Christian, one who receives by faith an infinite and atoning Saviour, and follows him as his supreme Master. In this particular, a visible church differs from the invisible, *all* the members of the latter being true believers in Christ. This company of true Christians must also be organized by a mutual covenant into a distinct and independent society, complete in itself, and acknowledging Christ as its only head. The only way in which such a voluntary society can be formed is by means of a mutual covenant, not necessarily formally written out, but at least acknowledged by the members. It must be so organized also as to be distinct and complete in itself, for we are giving the definition of *a church*, not of *a part* of a church. Consequently, there can be over it no judicatories, no king, priest, or bishop, to whom belongs either the whole or any part of the church authority; otherwise, without these, we should have only a fragment, and not the whole, of a church.[1] This definition likewise requires that the members of the church shall be so situated that they can conveniently meet statedly in *one place.* A church is a *local* organization, having for its object mutual and personal watch and care, and the regular congregating of its members for worship, and Christian observances. Such an organized collection of believers is a complete church. It needs nothing more in its structure to enable it to secure all its designed ends.

[1] "These [local] churches, *as they are churches*, are meet and able to attain the ends of churches. To say they are churches, and yet have not in themselves power to attain the ends of churches, is to speak contradictions, or to grant and deny the same thing in the same breath; for a church is nothing but such a society as hath power, ability, and fitness to attain those ends for which Christ hath ordained churches; that which hath so is a church, and that which hath not so is none. Men may, if they please, deny them to be churches, but then I know not where they will find any that are so . . . . . It is utterly foreign to the Scripture, and a monster unto antiquity that there should be *churches* with *a part, half, more or less,* of church power, and not the whole, neither in right nor exercise; or that there should be church officers, elders, presbyteries, or bishops, that should have a partiary power, half or a third part, or less, of that which entirely belongeth unto the office they hold. Let *one testimony* be given out of the Scripture, or that antiquity which we appeal unto, unto this purpose, and we shall cease our plea." — *John Owen's Works*, Vol. 15, p. 314, recent Edinburgh edition.

It is competent to transact all ecclesiastical business. It has authority to choose and place over itself its own officers, to discipline its own members, and to do all things necessary to secure the great ends of a church, subject only in these particulars to Christ, its head.

That this was the form of a church which Christ taught, is evident from his law of church discipline as laid down in the eighteenth chapter of Matthew. The Saviour in this passage incidentally gives a very clear description of a church. It is a representation of a church in complete and working order. According to this account of it, a church is, first, an *organized* society, organized by a mutual obligation on the part of its members, of brotherly watch and care. Therefore, secondly, it is a *local* society, a society of easy access and address: "Go tell the church." Thirdly, among all the members, as members, there is perfect equality; no one has more authority than another; they are all *brethren*, and Christ is their only head and lawgiver. Fourthly, the government of the church is in the hands of the brotherhood. After two private trials of an erring brother, if he is not gained, "tell it to the church;" that is, to the organized society of which each brother is a member, to the whole brotherhood; let them adjudicate upon the case. "Tell it to the *church*" cannot mean, tell it to the priest, bishop, or pope; it cannot mean, tell it to a session, or a presbytery, or any judiciary *above* the church. It means what it says: "Tell it to the *church*," the company of brethren with whom you are associated. No unprejudiced reader would think of any other meaning. This is the only common sense interpretation. Fifthly, the Saviour here teaches, with great emphasis, that the authority of the brotherhood is supreme and final. His language upon this point is the language of command: "*If he neglect to hear the church,* LET *him be unto thee as a heathen man and a publican.*" This *prohibits* an appeal from the decision of the local church to any other earthly tribunal. It is a *command* to terminate the case there. He is *to be* a heathen man and a publican *by the decision of the church*, whatever other authority may come in and claim to rejudge the case. And if a local church, after rendering its verdict, shall recognize any higher judicial authority than its own, whether it be that of an officer or a judicatory, a bishop or a presbytery, it violates this command of Christ. It refuses to terminate the trial at the point where *he commands* it to be terminated. It says to the Saviour, we will not *let* him be a heathen man and a publican if he neglects to hear us. Moreover, the Saviour, to prevent all mistake, particularly reminds the brethren of this local organization, that there is no church tribunal above their own save that of heaven. "Verily, I say unto you, whatsoever *ye* [you company of brethren], shall bind on earth shall be bound in heaven; and whatsoever *ye* shall loose on earth shall be loosed in heaven." Nothing, I apprehend, can be plainer than that the Saviour here teaches that the government of the church lies exclusively with the members, acting as a democratic body. If so, we have no right to say that the government of the church is not exclusively with the members, but is entirely or in part in the hands, either of certain officers or of certain judicatories above them. If the Saviour says that the authority of the members of a local church in an ecclesiastical matter is supreme and final, we have no right to say that it is not supreme and final. If the Saviour teaches that the local church is complete in itself, for all the purposes of a church, we have no right to say that it is not, and then go on to institute offices of a higher authority, or a cumbrous system of higher judicatories, to make it complete. There is great presumption in such a course. To say nothing of the commands of Christ, it is challenging his wisdom. For the Saviour does teach that a church is a *local* organization; that it is complete in itself; that the government of the church is in the hands of the mass of the members, acting as a purely democratic body; and that their authority in church government is supreme. And nowhere does he give the least intimation of any other kind or form of a visibly organized church.

The apostles, likewise, sanctioned and taught this form of a church, and no other. The radical principles of Congregationalism, and also its general spirit, are finely illustrated in the first instance of ecclesiastical action after the ascension of the Saviour. An apostle was to be chosen in the place of Judas; and we should of course expect that if the apostles were endowed with any superior ecclesiastical authority it would certainly now be made manifest. When could such authority be exercised, if not in filling a vacancy in their own number? But they expressly disclaim for themselves any such ecclesiastical supremacy, by submitting this most important election to the arbitration of a popular assembly of the disciples. There were "about one hundred and twenty" present at the meeting. Peter presided, distinctly announced the business, and called upon them to make an election. The meeting nominated two, Justus and Matthias. And, after prayer for divine guidance, "they," that is, the whole assembly of the disciples, acting as a purely democratic body, "gave forth their lots," or, as

Mosheim says this expression means, cast their votes, "and the lot," or the vote, "fell upon Matthias." There can be no doubt about the character of this ecclesiastical action; it was strictly popular, or democratic. The whole company of the disciples were called upon to make the election. "Without doubt," says Neander, "those expositors adopt the right view who suppose that not merely the apostles, but all the believers, were at that time assembled."[1] Now the argument is this: If even the apostles assumed no ecclesiastical supremacy over the mass of the brethren, what man, or body of men, is there, who can rightfully assume such supremacy? And if the apostles did not of themselves even fill a vacancy in their own number, but submitted the election to the vote of the assembled body of believers, what ecclesiastical business can there possibly be which may not be properly and rightfully done by such a popular assembly of the disciples? This certainly indicates that it is a most daring assumption for any man, or for any body of men, to pretend to exercise a higher ecclesiastical authority than that of the mass of the disciples acting as a democratic body, and it also plainly indicates that there is no necessity for any such

[1] Planting and Training of the Church, p. 19, note.

higher ecclesiastical authority. Thus in the very dawn of Christianity, and in the very first attempt made under the direction of the apostles to give it any visible organization, we find germinating those radical principles of Congregationalism, namely, the perfect equality of all the members of the Christian brotherhood as members, and the absolute supremacy, under Christ, of the authority of that brotherhood as an ecclesiastical body.

The next instance of ecclesiastical action under the direction of the apostles, of which we have any record, was the choice of seven deacons. It may possibly be objected to the argument just presented, that the election of an apostle was an extraordinary event, and that, therefore, it furnishes no precedent for ordinary ecclesiastical business. But we reply, first, that the fact that the business of electing an apostle was so extraordinary makes the argument all the stronger for Congregationalism, showing that by no possibility can there ever be any ecclesiastical business which may not be transacted by the brethren of a local church. And, secondly, we reply that the very next ecclesiastical action of the disciples was not extraordinary, and yet was conducted in precisely the same manner. The election was made, as before, by the whole body of believers. "The multitude of the disciples" were called together by the apostles. The business was distinctly laid before them, and they were requested to choose from among themselves seven men for the new office. "And the saying pleased the whole multitude; and they chose Stephen" and six others, and set them before the apostles, not to complete or to ratify the election, but simply that the apostles, as the servants of the church, might induct them into their office. Without question this was a strictly popular election; the apostles thus again teaching that the power of appointing men to office in the church was not in their hands, nor in the hands of any man, or body of men, above the church, but exclusively in the hands of the brotherhood of the disciples. "It were well," says John Owen, in commenting upon the manner of this election, "if some would consider how the apostles at that time treated that multitude of the people, which is so much now despised and utterly excluded from all concern in church affairs but what consists in servile subjection . . . . . It is marvellous to me, that any who would be thought to succeed them in any part of their trust and office should dare to depart from the example set before them by the Holy Ghost in them, preferring their own ways and inventions above it. I shall ever judge that there is more safety in a strict adherence unto this apostolical practice and example, than in a compliance with all the canons of councils or churches afterward."[1]

Again, even in the presence of the apostles, the elders or ministers of the churches were chosen either by the vote, or with the sanction, of the brotherhood. We read in the fourteenth chapter of the Acts: "And when they [the apostles] had ordained them elders in every church," etc. The manner of the appointment of these elders is to be determined by the meaning of the original word, rendered in this passage "ordained." This word never means to ordain, in the modern signification of the term; it never means to set apart, or to consecrate, by the imposition of hands. It means, primarily, to appoint, or to elect, by an *uplifting* of the hands, or by a popular vote; and, then, it means simply to choose, to appoint. The apostles, then, chose or appointed elders in every church. And this may mean, either that they presided at the meeting and made the election by receiving the suffrages of the brethren and announcing the result, or that they alone made the election. And even if we adopt the latter meaning, there is no probability that the election was made without the sanction of the brethren. An apostle even was chosen by popular vote. The seven deacons were elected in the same manner;

[1] Owen's Works, Vol. XVI. pp. 59, 60.

and these facts of themselves render it altogether improbable that ministers would be placed over the churches without even the approval of the brethren. The same word, rendered in this passage to ordain, is used, in the eighth chapter of Second Corinthians, to express the fact of a popular election of a delegate. This delegate was — not ordained — but "*chosen of the churches.*" And such would have been the rendering of the word in the fourteenth of Acts, but for the Episcopal correction, substituting *ordain* for *choose.* The translations, previous to that of King James's bishops, affirm that the appointment was made "*by election.*" The meaning, therefore, obviously is, that the elders were appointed either by a popular election or by the expressed sanction of the people; and either of these methods implies the sovereignty of the local church.[1]

Again, the apostles taught the independency of the local church, and the supremacy of its authority under Christ, by the manner in which they directed that the discipline of the church should be administered. The case of the incestuous person, of whom Paul wrote in the fifth chapter of his first epistle to the Corinthians, is a notable example: "When ye *are gathered together,*" the apostle says to the Corinthian church, this wicked member is to be delivered

[1] See Appendix, note B.

over to Satan. It was to be done by the whole body of the church. Paul censures them for not having done this before, which he could not do unless the authority to administer discipline, even in its severest form, was fully in their hands. "Do not *ye*," he says, "judge them that are within? . . . . . Therefore put away from among yourselves that wicked person." The apostle afterwards speaks of this excommunication as having been an act of the church. The punishment, he says, "was inflicted of many;" that is, by the *majority*, showing that the sentence was passed by a popular vote. According to Paul, then, the power of administering discipline is in the hands of the brethren of the local church, and in the exercise of it they are to act as a strictly independent and democratic body. And we have no reason to believe that the views of Paul upon this point were peculiar. All the rest of the apostles, undoubtedly, adopted and taught the same mode of procedure.

Thus the apostles, by the manner in which they filled a vacancy in their own number; by the manner in which, under their direction, the election of deacons and pastors was made; and also by the way in which they ordered the discipline of the church to be conducted, teach the same form of a church as that which is so clearly indicated in the Saviour's

3*

rule of discipline. It was the practice, even of the apostles, to assume no ecclesiastical authority over the churches, no veto power over their action; but always to demean themselves as their servants. They consulted with them, counselled and persuaded them, as if the supreme authority, or the whole responsibility of final action, was with them. They thus plainly declare, that the sovereign power is vested in the brethren of the local church; that these brethren are not only to have part in all church action, but also are amply competent for the performance of every kind of ecclesiastical business; that with them are even "the keys of the kingdom," the sole, and therefore supreme authority under Christ, to open and to shut, to bind and to loose.

The following facts likewise, in this connection, have an irresistible force. The apostles addressed their epistles to particular local churches, as if these were the only kind of which they had any knowledge. They enjoined duties upon no other ecclesiastical organization. Much of their writings consist of directions respecting the care and management of local churches; but nowhere do they give one direction in respect to the care or management of an organized collection of them. They gave directions for the appointment of no church officers except those of distinct, independent churches. They invariably denominated a bishop's charge *a church;* never *churches.* There is not the least intimation that they ever thought of such a thing as a modern diocese. Even in John's vision of the church triumphant no bishops appear, but only elders or presbyters. Such a thing as a diocesan bishop, either in heaven or on earth, seems never to have entered the minds of the apostles. Neither did they give any instructions respecting any ecclesiastical tribunal higher than that of a local church. The inspired founders of Christianity had no knowledge of any thing corresponding to modern presbyteries, synods, and general assemblies. All these statements commend themselves at once as true to every mind familiar with the New Testament. And these, and many other similar facts that might be mentioned, establish the truth, that the apostles, as well as Christ, sanctioned and taught that form of a church which we now denominate Congregational, and that they sanctioned and taught no other.

2. In the second place, the officers of a church, such as were authorized by the writers of the New Testament, were the officers of a Congregational church, and were of two orders only — ministers and deacons. It is true, that, in the origin of Christianity, there was a distinct *class* of *men* in the churches; that is, the apostles. But these did not constitute a

distinct *order* of church *officers*. Obviously they were appointed to their extraordinary station for the specific purpose of being witnesses to the resurrection of Christ, and of aiding, by their inspiration and other miraculous powers, the introduction of Christianity into the world.[1] That purpose having been

[1] "They [the apostles]," says Neander, "stand as the medium of communication between Christ and the whole Christian church, to transmit his word and his spirit through all ages. In this respect the church must ever continue to acknowledge her dependence upon them, and to own their rightful authority. Their authority and power can be delegated to none other. But the service which the apostles themselves sought to confer was to transmit to men the word and the spirit of the Lord, and by this means to establish independent Christian communities. These communities, when once established, they refused to hold in a state of slavish dependence upon themselves. Their object was, in the spirit of the Lord, to make the churches free and independent of their guidance. To the churches their language was: 'Ye beloved, ye are made free; be ye the servants of no man.' The churches were taught to govern themselves. All the members were made to coöperate together as organs of one spirit. . . . . Thus they, whose prerogative it was to rule among the brethren, demeaned themselves as the servants of Christ and his church." — *Primitive Church*, by Dr. L. Coleman, Introduction, pp. 18, 19.

With regard to the arguments that are used to prove that Timothy and Titus and the angels of the seven churches in Asia were church officers of the same rank as the apostles, or at least

fully accomplished, the class, of course, ceased. Thus we now have authority for only two orders of officers.

belonged to an order far above that of presbyters or ministers, we deem them too obviously specious to require any formal refutation. Half of the "charges" now given to Congregational ministers at the time of their ordination, two centuries hence will prove as conclusively that half of the ministers of our denomination in 1857 belonged to an order of officers higher than that of the other ministers, as the instructions of Paul to Timothy and Titus now prove that they belonged to an order of officers higher in authority than that of presbyters. If they were evangelists, that gave them no more church *authority* than belongs to the office of elder or minister. The apostles gave ecclesiastical authority to no church officers, but expressly affirmed that they were to be considered as *servants* of the church. They taught that the sovereignty was exclusively in the hands of the brotherhood of the local church. The Episcopalians themselves, generally, have now abandoned the claims of episcopacy, on the ground that there was a distinction in the primitive church between bishop and presbyter, but defend their claims on the ground that there was a grade of officers, not designated in the Scriptures, composed of the apostles and Timothy and Titus and the angels of the seven churches, from which the modern bishop can trace his descent. The whole fabric of episcopacy is thus made to rest upon the supposition of a grade of officers that has no name in the New Testament, and that is not even described. "Yet the modern bishop," says Dr. Coleman, "with astonishing credulity, traces back his spiritual lineage, we had almost said, through a thousand generations, in strange uncertainty all the while to

First, we have ministers, or pastors. Those who held this office in the time of the apostles were

whom he shall at last attach himself, or with whom claim kindred. If Peter fails him, he flies to Paul, to James, to Timothy, to Titus, to the angel of the church, to — he knows not whom. He is, however, a legitimate descendant and successor of some apostolical bishop; he is sure of that. But that bishop — nobody knows who he is, or what precisely his office may have been." With regard to all attempts to demonstrate such a thing as an apostolical succession in an unbroken line of bishops down to the present time, we agree with the remark of Rev. Albert Barnes, that "nothing that assumes to be a grave matter is more ridiculous or contemptible than the attempt, with a grave face, to exhibit such a demonstration." No man on earth can prove such a succession. Neander affirms that, "beyond a doubt, presbyters were accustomed to ordain in the ages immediately succeeding the apostles." Another scholar, not an "irreverent dissenter," but a "devoted son" of the Episcopal church and "a distinguished layman" of England, asserts that "Episcopacy, in the modern acceptation of the term, did not exist in the time of the apostles; and that, however expedient and desirable such an institution might be, it cannot plead the sanction of apostolic appointment or example. It may be difficult to fix the period exactly when the episcopate was first recognized as a distinct *order* in the church, and when the consecration of bishops, as such, came to be in general use; clearly not, I think, when St. Jerome wrote, [Jerome died A. D. 426.] "Thus much at least is certain, namely, that the government of each church, *including the ordination of ministers*, was at first in the hands of the presbytery." This Episcopalian author, with Neander and other learned historians,

called elders, bishops, overseers, presbyters, teachers, guides; all these terms being used to designate one office; just as we now use the terms minister and pastor to designate, not two distinct orders in office, but the same order. It will be seen at once, that it is of primary importance, in establishing the divine authority of our system of church government, to prove that all these terms are names applied to persons holding, not so many different offices, but one and the same office. But, if we begin to make any distinction, it will be very difficult for any one to show why we should not make as many distinct offices as there are distinct terms. If we make a distinction between elders and ministers, why not

believes that a presbytery in the primitive churches was simply a board, composed of the officers of a single local church. After showing that the first bishop must have received his ordination from presbyters, and therefore "could of necessity receive no more than it was in their power to bestow," he proceeds as follows: "At whatever period, therefore, it [Episcopacy] was adopted, and with whatever uniformity it might be continued, and whatever of value or even authority it might hence acquire, still, as an apostolical institution, it has none. There is a gap which never can be filled; or, rather, the link by which the whole must be suspended is wanting, and can never be supplied. There can be no apostolical succession of that which had no apostolical existence." — *Bowdler's Letters*, as cited by Dr. Coleman in his Primitive Church, pp. 196, 197.

between ministers and bishops? Or, if we make a distinction between bishops and ministers, why not between ministers and elders? Accordingly we find, that, in one of our denominations, an elder is merely a layman, who is a member of a Church Session; while in other denominations an elder is a minister or presbyter; while in other denominations still, the office of minister, or presbyter, is distinct from that of bishop, the latter being invested with a superior authority.

Now the simple historical fact is, it was the practice of the primitive Christians to have, if they pleased, several ministers, elders, presbyters, bishops, or whatever they were called, to each church. They might have one or more; there was no limit given to the number by the apostles. According to this custom, many of the first churches of New England, though small and feeble, supported two able ministers. Many Congregational churches now have more than one. One Congregational church in New England, at the present time, has five. In the time of the primitive Christians, these several ministers of a church would form a board of ministers, elders, presbyters, or bishops, differing from each other, not in official rank or authority, but only in personal attainments and character, one having perhaps peculiar gifts for ruling, another for teaching, another for exhortation; and so this board, or *presbytery*, as they were then called, would naturally divide the labor of their common office between them, according to their several gifts, that each might exercise his own. Hence they would have ruling elders, and teaching elders, and exhorting elders; all these having the same rank in office, or the same authority; all being alike *elders*, or, in other words, differing from each other, not in the offices which they held, but only as they divided among themselves the work of one and the same office. Nowhere is there the least intimation given that any one elder had any preëminence over another. Indeed, it is absurd to suppose that a *ruling* elder would be inferior in authority to a *teaching* elder. The qualifications of all elders, and the manner of their call and ordination, were the same. Consequently, every person, officially designated by this term, filled the highest office in the church under Christ. And so we find that the elders are spoken of, in the New Testament, as if they were the ministers or pastors of the churches. The apostles more usually called the ministers of a church its elders. They appointed "elders in every church," and the duties enjoined upon these were the duties of ministers. If these elders were not the ministers of those churches, those churches had no ministers. An elder was also a bishop. The qualifications of both are declared to be the same. No duty was enjoined upon a bishop that was not enjoined upon an elder. We are distinctly informed that it was usual to have several bishops over one church, as in Philippians 1: 1; Acts 20: 28; but nowhere in the New Testament is there any intimation that one bishop was placed over several churches. The bishops spoken of in Philippians 1: 1 had only deacons associated with them, consequently they were the elders of that church. The elders of the church at Ephesus are called overseers, that is, bishops.[1] In Titus 1: 5–7 we are again informed that elders are bishops, the terms being used interchangeably to designate the same office. In 1 Timothy iii. the offices of bishops and deacons are spoken of as if they were the only offices in a church. In 1 Peter 5: 2, 3, the apostle, as an elder, exhorts *the elders* to feed the flock of God, "*taking the oversight thereof*," or as the word in the original means, *acting as bishops.* A bishop, then, is an elder, and only an elder, and an elder is a minister; and a board of elders or ministers, officiating in a single local church, is a board of bishops.* There is no authority in the New Testament for making any distinction between a board of elders and a board

[1] Acts 20: 17 and 28. The word here translated *overseers* is the same word which is elsewhere translated *bishops.*

of presbyters, or between a board of presbyters and a board of bishops; nor for making any distinction between a board of elders and a board of elders and presbyters. All such distinctions are of human origin. Nor is there any authority in the New Testament for judicial and legislative bodies, made up of presbyters, and delegates falsely called elders, from several churches. If there is, why has it not been shown? Where is the page in the New Testament that gives any authority for a modern Church Session; composed of the ministers of the church, and certain of the brethren chosen to officiate for life and called elders; and transacting all the business of the church except that of their own election, and also that which is transacted by higher judicatories? Where is the scriptural authority for a modern Presbytery, composed of ministers and delegates from several Church Sessions, and exercising a judicial authority superior to that of the local church? The only Presbytery, known to the apostles and primitive Christians, was that composed of the presbyters or pastors of a single church. And so where is the scriptural warrant for the Synod and the General Assembly? Would any candid reader of the New Testament ever receive the remotest hint of such a ponderous system of connected judicatories, all the repositories of a judicial, legislative, and executive power higher than that of the local church?

The second order of officers in the church is that of deacons. This is a distinct office, having its own distinct duties, and is the only other office of divine appointment in the church. It is the duty of the deacons to attend to the collection of the alms of the church, and to the distribution of them to the poor, and in other things so to assist the elders or ministers that they shall not be obliged to "leave the word of God, and serve tables."

Now it should be particularly noticed, that both ministers and deacons are officers of single, local churches. There is no provision of officers made for any other kind of a church. Nothing whatever is said about the construction, or the official appointments, or the tribunals, or the management of a church, made up of a collection of churches; and, therefore, every such ecclesiastical organization is merely human. Moreover, both of these classes of officers which we have mentioned grew out of the local church. They were appointed to their office by the members. Thus the officers were not *placed over* the church, but were *chosen by* the church. They had not the government or the authority of the church in their hands. They were simply the *servants* of the church, for the Lord's sake. They had no right to regard themselves as "lords over God's heritage," and were expressly forbidden to claim any such church authority.[1] Thus the offices in the church were of such a nature as to be in perfect conformity with the judicial and legislative supremacy of the brotherhood.

3. In the third place, the relation of the primitive churches to each other was that of distinct, complete churches, united only by a common faith, and by mutual Christian love and fellowship; and this is the mutual relation of Congregational churches. The first Christian churches were independent. No one of them was under the control or authority of all, or any, of the rest; nor was any one of them under the control or authority of any officer or judicatory placed over a part, or all, of the churches. They all stood upon the same level, each a distinct, complete, independent church, and had no control over each other, except through the persuasive influences of Christian character and love. They were not independent, in the sense that they paid no regard to each other. They were united by the strongest of all ties, Christian love, and were ever ready to perform, voluntarily, all those acts of mutual kindness and sympathy which would naturally be prompted by such love. It is on this account that the word *Congregational* is more appropriate

[1] 1 Peter 5: 3.

than the word *Independent*, as descriptive of the primitive form of church government. There is nothing in the nature of this divine form of a church to prevent one church asking advice or assistance of another. On the contrary, there is every thing in the nature of the union of the churches to encourage this. Hence the propriety of ecclesiastical councils composed of messengers, sent by the several churches whose advice or assistance has been asked. But these councils can have no permanent organization; neither can they have any ecclesiastical authority over a church. They cannot ordain a minister, nor dismiss one; they cannot excommunicate a brother, nor restore one already excommunicated; they cannot perform any ecclesiastical business for the church which has called them, unless requested or permitted to do it by the members of that church. They can simply consult, advise, assist. They have no judicial or legislative authority whatever.[1] One church may also ask for the advice or the opinion of the whole brotherhood of another church in settling some difficult point in doctrine or discipline. We have an account of such a conference as this between two churches, in the fifteenth chapter of Acts; the *brethren* of the church at Antioch sending a disputed question by chosen

[1] See Appendix, note C.

messengers to the apostles and elders and church at Jerusalem; and "the apostles and elders, *with the whole church*" at Jerusalem, sending back their judgment in the case. There was nothing in this that had the remotest resemblance to a permanent and superior judicatory over the churches. It was simply a conference of two churches, and it never met but once. No such voluntary and friendly intercourse between the churches can interfere, in the least degree, with their individual completeness and independence. Neither is there any thing in the nature of this scriptural form of a church to prevent the ministers of several churches uniting, if they please, to form an association for mutual improvement, and for consultation respecting the interests of the churches, but not to exercise over them any governmental authority. There is nothing, either, in this primitive constitution of the church, to prevent the members of several churches uniting their prayers and labors in carrying forward some enterprise of Christian benevolence. They may even form a society to accomplish such an object, but not to exercise any authority over the local churches. No organization that takes any thing away from the *completeness* of a local church, or in any degree forms a complement to it, or to its authority, has any warrant in Scripture. Where, in the New Testament, is there any authority for any church judicatory higher than that of the brethren of a local church, whether you call that judicatory a convention, a presbytery, a synod, or assembly? No such thing was known in the time of the apostles. There was no such connection of the churches, no such subordination of them to superior tribunals. There were no such material ligaments binding them all together, and, at the sacrifice of their individual completeness and independence, building up a great centralized system of church government. There is not the least intimation in the Bible of any such general government extending its supervision and control over all or any of the churches. And these facts, we affirm, are decisive of the question before us. The primitive churches were distinct, complete, independent, local, or, as we now denominate them, Congregational churches.[1]

[1] Looking upon the primitive churches as thus all independent, each complete in itself, what relation would a centralized church, springing up among them, have sustained to all the rest? If, for instance, the churches of Asia, or those of Judea, immediately after the death of the apostles, had banded together and adopted another form of church government, and organized themselves into a Presbyterian, or a Methodist, or an Episcopal church, what would have been their position among the churches of Christendom? Most certainly it would have been sectarian and schismatic. And why is not any subsequent rise of a centralized

Indeed, so far as any argument from the Bible for a system of church government is concerned, there is no tenable stopping-place between Congregationalism and Popery. If one degree of authority should be exercised over a local church, then it is easy to prove that two degrees should be; and if two degrees should be exercised, then should three; and if three, then four; and so on to absolute despotism. And it makes no difference whether this superior authority to that of a local church is embodied in an officer or in a judicatory. If there should be a diocesan officer over the bishops or ministers of local churches, then there should be a national officer over the diocesan, and, finally, a pope over all the world. And so, if there should be a permanent church judicatory invested with superior authority over the members, then, for the same reason, there should be another judicatory over that. That is, if there should be a session over the church, there should be a presbytery over the session, and then a synod over the presbytery, and then an assembly

church equally sectarian and schismatic? Why is not every consolidated church, of whatever kind, organizing itself, as every such church does, on a new and more or less unscriptural plan, and fencing itself off from all other churches, a schism in the body of Christ? And why is not Popery the greatest schism in the history of Christianity?

over the synod; and no one can give any reason whatever from the Bible, why the line of judicatories should stop with the assembly. By the same reasoning, if a church should be governed by an oligarchy of elders, it should be governed by the monarchy of a pope. Nowhere along the line between Congregationalism and Absolutism is there any one position that can be taken and defended from the Bible any better than any other. There is no logical stopping-place between the local church and Rome; hence the drift from the less centralized systems of church government is always towards ecclesiastical despotism.[1] Even the mildest

[1] "Associationism," says Dr. Emmons, "leads to Consociationism; Consociationism leads to Presbyterianism; Presbyterianism leads to Episcopacy; Episcopacy leads to Roman Catholicism; and Roman Catholicism is an ultimate fact." — Emmons's Works, Vol. I. Memoirs, p. 135.

"There are but two steps," says John Wise, "from an aristocracy to a monarchy, and from thence but one to a tyranny; an able and standing force, and an ill nature, *ipso facto*, turn an absolute monarch into a tyrant; this is obvious among the Roman Cæsars, and through the world. And all these direful transmutations are easier in church affairs (from the different qualities of the things) than in civil states." — Vindication of N. E. Churches, p. 41.

"Far distant be the day when the Consociations of Connecticut shall appear in the mother country among our Congre-

of these systems can form no permanent union of any kind with Congregationalism. A breach will soon begin, and inevitably continue to widen, as, by an inherent and uncontrollable tendency, they recoil from the contact. There must forever be a palpable and fixed line of demarcation between the people's *governing* and *being governed.* Inside of this line is the primitive, scriptural church; but outside all is adrift. If the brethren of a local church *govern,* they stand fast in the position of the primitive churches; but the moment they suffer themselves in any degree to *be governed,* they leave that position and begin to travel towards Rome.[1] In those churches that are drifting towards absolute despotism, reformers will arise now and then, as they have already frequently arisen, who will seek to stem the increasing power and tyranny of the *few,* and re-

gational churches! Unlike the stated associations formed among us in most countries, they lead to Presbyterianism." — Ecclesiastical Polity of the New Testament, by Samuel Davidson, D. D. p. 271.

"If you were to take the *great mass of the people* of England, you would find a burst of righteous indignation against them (the Tractarians). They would say, 'If we are to have Popery, let us have honest old Popery, at once. If you are right, you do not go far enough; and if you are wrong, you go too far.'" — Rev. Mr. Stowell, cited by Dr. Coleman in his Primitive Church, p. 85.

[1] See Appendix, Note D.

store to the *people* their divine but lost rights. In all great religious reformations in consolidated churches, the tendency is always back towards the primitive mode of church government. Under the influences of the Reformation of Geneva and Scotland, converted men passed at once from Popery to Presbyterianism, a long step towards the simple, scriptural form of a church. Under the same kind of influence, Luther passed, at one stride, from Popery to Congregationalism. And no man, who conscientiously takes the Bible for his infallible rule of practice, as did the Pilgrims, can logically or morally avoid coming over to their system, though it be through fire and blood, and a second exile for freedom to worship God. For it must for ever stand an immovable fact, that the brotherhood of a local church is the highest judicial and executive tribunal known in the New Testament. If we have a right to have any tribunal higher than this, we have a right to have any tribunal we please, and any form of church government whatever, according to our own taste or fancy, or ideas of expediency, entirely regardless of the Scriptures.

Here we might rest the case. The argument, which we have briefly sketched, proves, beyond all reasonable controversy, that the church polity of the Pilgrims was that instituted by Christ and the apostles. The chief recommendation of Congregationalism is its scripturalness. In the language of a learned English divine: "It rests on the immovable basis of the Divine Word. It challenges inquiry because of its sacred foundation. Whoever undertakes to overthrow it, must assail it chiefly with weapons drawn from the Bible."

But if we would make what is certain doubly certain, there is still an historical argument of great force, that brings us to the same conclusion. All the accredited evidence that can be gathered from other sources than the New Testament goes to prove that the churches of the primitive Christians were Congregational churches. Dr. John Owen lays down, and, with the most elaborate research, establishes the proposition, "*that in no approved writers, for the space of two hundred years after Christ, is there any mention made of any other organical, visibly professing church, but that only which is parochial or congregational.*"[1] The most accredited church historians render similar testimony. "We are disposed to believe," says Neander, "that the church was at first composed entirely of members standing on an equality with one another, and that the apostles alone held a higher rank, and exercised a

[1] Owen's Works, Vol. XV. p. 277.

directing influence over the whole."[1] Again he says: "As regards the relation in which the presbyters stood to the communities [churches], they were not designed to exercise absolute authority, but to act as presiding officers, and guides of an ecclesiastical republic; to conduct all things, with the coöperation of the communities, as their ministers, and not their masters."[2]

"The principal voice," says Mosheim, "was that of the *people*, or of the whole body of Christians; for even the apostles themselves inculcated, by their example, that nothing of any moment was to be done or determined on but with the knowledge and consent of the brotherhood." "The assembled people elected their own rulers and teachers, or by their free consent received such as were nominated to them. . . . In a word, the people did every thing that is proper for those in whom the *supreme power* of the community is vested. . . . Among all members of the church, of whatever class or condition, there was the most perfect equality."[3] Again, he says of the churches of the first century: "All the churches, in those primitive times, were *independent* bodies; or none of them subject to the jurisdic-

[1] Neander's Planting and Training of the Church, p. 33.

[2] Neander's Church History, Vol. I. p. 189.

[3] Mosheim's Ecclesiastical History, Murdock's Translation, Vol. I. p. 68.

tion of any other. For, though the churches which were founded by the apostles themselves frequently had the honor shown them to be consulted in difficult and doubtful cases, yet they had no judicial authority, no control, no power of giving laws. On the contrary, it is clear as the noonday, that all Christian churches had *equal rights*, and were in all respects on a footing of equality. Nor does there appear, in this first century, any vestige of that *consociation* of the churches of the same province which gave rise to *ecclesiastical councils* and to *metropolitans*." [1] Of the second century he says: "During a great part of this century, all the churches continued to be, as at first, *independent* of each other, or were connected by no consociations or confederations. Each church was a kind of small, independent republic, governing itself by its own laws, enacted, or at least sanctioned, by the people." [2]

Still again we find this reliable historian saying: "Although all the churches were, in the first age of Christianity, united together in one common bond of faith and love, and were, in every respect, ready to promote the interests and welfare of each other by a reciprocal interchange of good offices, yet, with regard to government and internal economy, every

[1] Mosheim's Ecclesiastical History, Vol. I. p. 72.

[2] Ibid. p. 116.

individual church considered itself as an independent community, none of them ever looking, in these respects, beyond the circle of its own members for assistance, or recognizing any sort of external influence or authority. Neither in the New Testament nor in any ancient document whatever do we find any thing recorded, from whence it might be inferred that any of the minor churches were at all dependent on, or looked up for direction to, those of greater magnitude or consequence; on the contrary, several things occur therein, which put it out of all doubt that every one of them enjoyed the same rights, and was considered as being on a footing of the most perfect equality with the rest. Indeed it cannot, — I will not say be proved, but even be made to appear probable, from any testimony, divine or human, that in this age it was the practice for several churches to enter into and maintain amongst themselves, that sort of association which afterwards came to subsist amongst the churches of almost every province."[1]

"They [the apostles]," says Dr. Coleman, "instituted no external form of union or confederation between [the churches] of different towns or provinces; nor within the first century of the Christian era can any trace of such a confederacy, whether

[1] Mosheim's Historical Commentaries on Christianity in the First Three Centuries, Vol. I. p. 196.

diocesan or conventional, be detected on the page of history. The diocesan, metropolitan, and patriarchal forms of organization belong to a later age. The idea of a holy catholic church, one and indivisible, had not yet arisen in the church, nor had it assumed any outward form of union. Wherever converts to Christianity were multiplied, they formed themselves into a church, under the guidance of their religious teachers, for the enjoyment of Christian ordinances. But each individual church constituted an independent and separate community. The society was purely voluntary, and every church so constituted was strictly independent of all others in the conduct of its worship, the admission of its members, the exercise of its discipline, the choice of its officers, and the entire management of its affairs. They were, in a word, independent republics."[1]

Now this was the church polity of the Pilgrim Fathers. They took for their model the churches of the New Testament. They went back to the primitive Christians, and copied, as closely as possible, their form of church government. It is sometimes said that the Rev. John Robinson, the godly pastor of the Leyden-Plymouth Church, was the author of Congregationalism. But no. "It was instituted,"

[1] The Primitive Church, by Coleman, p. 47. — See Appendix, Note E.

says John Cotton, "and practised in the first ages of Christianity, and our Saviour himself is the true author of this first ecclesiastical state of the church." "The primitive churches of the apostolic age," says Gov. Winslow, "were the pattern which Mr. Robinson had in his eye." It may seem strange that this primitive and scriptural form of the Christian church should have been disregarded for so many centuries, and have been revived again only two centuries and a half ago. But ecclesiastical corruption and despotism crushed it out. The world was not worthy of it; and, therefore, for more than thirteen centuries in the world, it was like its Great Author, who had not where to lay his head. The Pilgrims searched for the account of it in the New Testament, and found it; and, believing that the form of a church which they thus found and adopted was divine, the only form which Christ designed to leave, the only form which the apostles taught by word or practice; and, therefore, believing that it differed from all human societies or organizations in this, that it *was divine*, and that no man or body of men on earth, not even the members of a local church themselves, had any authority to alter its constitution, its ordinances, or its offices, Christ being its only lawgiver, they labored and suffered and prayed for it amidst persecutions and in exile, until they entered into their rest. They bequeathed their hard-earned liberty to revive and enjoy this first and divine form of a Christian church to their descendants. The Congregationalism of New England is the church polity of the Pilgrims. And it is this, my hearers, your own church order, so precious in itself and in its history; the church order of the Pilgrim Fathers; the church order of Christ and the apostles; that you are called upon to-day to give to your country.

II. But, in the second place, the divine origin of the church polity of the Pilgrims is not the only argument with which I would commend it to your most favorable regard. If it is divine, it doubtless has an inherent fitness for its ends worthy of its divinity. If it is the church order of Christ and the apostles, we might reasonably expect that it would have intrinsic excellences and aptitudes, as a system of church government, peculiar to itself, and consequently be endowed with a power for good in the world, preëminent, and worthy of its Author. I have time to mention only a few of these excellences, and shall select those which seem to me best fitted to impress our minds with the great wisdom, and the duty, of more earnest and systematic effort, on the part of our churches, to extend this apostolic and primitive system of church government throughout our country.

1. In the first place, this divine church polity is peculiarly fitted to reach and elevate the masses of the people. Congregationalism is founded upon the principle, that the church is made for the many, and not merely for the few. As the Saviour said of the Sabbath, so we may say of the church; the church was made for man, and not man for the church. But when the great mass of the members are made the mere slaves of a great and imposing church system, or of a church oligarchy installed over them, the church is no longer made for the masses, but they are made for the church. The primary design of this divine Institution is thus defeated. That which was wisely fitted to promote the highest good of the many is so perverted as to become a ponderous machine for making the many subserve the ambitious and selfish interests of the few. The church polity of the Pilgrims prevents any approach to such a perversion of this divine Institution, by placing the entire government of each local church in the hands of its members. And it is just this feature of this church polity that makes it so admirably fitted to develop the natural powers, as well as the Christian character, of every member, and so to elevate the whole mass of the brethren intellectually and spiritually. The church is thus made to subserve the real interests of its members. It calls them all up,

even the very humblest of them, to an arena of high and responsible personal action. The government of a church of Christ is in their hands. The acts of a church are often more momentous than the acts of a nation; and no church action can be taken except by the suffrages of the members; and thus the very lowliest as well as the most gifted brother is called upon to deliberate upon every question coming before them, to decide independently and definitely upon the expediency or inexpediency, the rightness or wrongness, of the action proposed, and to render his judgment accordingly. No person can be received into the church until all the members have had an opportunity to ascertain and weigh well the evidence of his fitness for the communion of the saints, and to make objections, if they shall deem it best. If any weighty matter of discipline is brought before the church, the very weakest as well as the strongest brother is called upon to prepare his mind and his heart for the high duty before him, and then to adjudicate upon the case to the best of his ability, faithfully and righteously pronouncing his judgment, responsible to Christ alone. In all this a silent but mighty influence is brought to bear upon each individual member, developing independence of thought, independence of action, manliness and force of character. This wise system of church government is wonderfully fitted to work upon *mind.* It was ordained by him who made the soul, and who knows its worth. It does not treat men as if they were fit only to be parts of a machine, and could move only as they are moved by some all-controlling mechanical power above them. It treats men as if they *were* men, — as if they were endowed with free-will and immortal being, and must stand before God, each one for himself alone, and give an account of his own deeds done in the body; and therefore it rigorously and reverently conforms to the established laws of free and immortal mind. It was the profound remark of John Owen, that "churches may *inform* the *minds* of men, but they *cannot enforce* them." And then he adds, that, if the *members* of any church do not act freely, as they judge is their duty, and best for them, to act, "they therein differ not much from a herd of creatures that are called by another name." This divine church order proves its divinity by treating men as our Saviour treated them when he laid down his life to save them. It magnifies their worth. It especially exalts the redeemed of the Lord, and orders all its conduct towards them as if they were those little ones, whom if any one offend, "it were better for him that a mill-stone were hanged about his neck, and that he were drowned in the depth of the sea." It raises them, one and all, in official position. It makes every brother alike responsible for the most momentous trusts. It places every member in a royal office, and calls upon him to administer his office, responsible only to the Great Head of the church. It intrusts every brother alike with the watch and care of the body of Christ. The poorest, lowliest brother holds this office equally with the most wealthy or gifted. And it is a regal office that he fills, for there is no one above him on earth. The officers of the church even are only his servants. The very highest of them is only *his minister*. *He*, that humble church-member, is in the regal office; yea, more than a regal office, for no earthly potentate has the care of a world; and a single soul is of more worth than a world. And thus, in this divine form of the church, every man is made his own king and his own priest, and therefore all the members are kings and priests unto God; which led the great historian Neander, as he pondered upon this primitive form of the church, to pronounce it "*a divine kingdom of priests.*"

A church polity which thus elevates the mass of the members, inclines them to fit themselves, by every means in their power, to meet the responsibilities of their elevated position. The committee room, the conference room, the church and prayer-meeting, the watch and care for which they are responsible, make them feel the need of developing their powers, both of mind and of heart, to the utmost degree, that they may discharge properly the high duties that have been devolved upon them. And then, from this increased mental culture and elevation of character in the church, goes out a mighty influence, reaching through all the community around, and promoting generally intelligence and virtue. Such a church polity goes right down among the masses of the people, and, by a thousand silent and winding influences, tends to make them, one and all, feel that they are called upon to take, and may take, a high position in life; and thus they are stimulated to prepare themselves to occupy it. The very presence of such a church polity shows the necessity of the general education of the people; and therefore it has happened that wherever the church order of the Pilgrims has gone, the school-house has gone, and well endowed academies and colleges have sprung up on every hand, as by enchantment. It is a significant historical fact, that New England, the great seat of this church order, has been foremost of all the world in efforts to promote popular education, and in the success which has attended them.[1] It was here, under the influ-

[1] "In New England, so admirable is the school system, and so deserving of all imitation, that only one person over twenty

ence of Congregationalism, that the experiment was made, for the first time in the world, of establishing

years of age is incapable of reading and writing in every four hundred of the number of native whites. In the South and South-west, the number is one in about twelve; and in the territories, one in about six; in the slave-holding States, one in twelve; in the non-slaveholding, one in forty; in the whole Union, one in about twenty-two." — United States Census, 1850. From the same source, we learn that the proportion of scholars at school to the whole population, is, in Maine, one scholar to every 3.1 persons; in Prussia, one scholar to 6.2 persons; in Great Britain, one to 8.5; in France, one to 10.5; in Austria, one to 13.7; in Russia, one to 50. Or, to give a still more definite illustration, taken from another source, the proportion of white adults over twenty years of age who cannot read and write is, "in Connecticut, 1 to every 568; in North Carolina, 1 to every 7. In Vermont, 1 to every 473; in South Carolina, 1 to every 17." — New Englander for 1857, p. 641. "Boston," — said Dr. Horner, President of the Geological Society in London, in conversation with the late Prof. B. B. Edwards, — "Boston is doing more than the whole of England for popular education." This inherent tendency of Congregationalism, as a powerful stimulative to popular education, developed itself very early in New England. "It was ever the custom," says Mr. Bancroft, in his History of the United States, "and it soon became the law, in Puritan New England, that 'none of the brethren shall suffer so much barbarism in their families as not to teach their children and apprentices so much learning as may enable them perfectly to read the English tongue.'" And again he says: "In these measures [of education], especially in the laws establishing common schools,

free schools. General thrift and enterprise have followed in the wake of this universal intellectual culture, and, therefore, the praise of New England is in all the world.

Nor is this system less adapted to the higher than the lower classes in society. It would be strange indeed if a church polity, which is divinely fitted to the intellectual and moral constitution of man, should not be able to carry him on from any degree of elevation in the scale of being which he will be likely to reach in his earthly life. It has shown itself to be peculiarly congenial to great minds and generous natures. "Two centuries ago," says an English writer, "Congregationalism could make mention of knights and nobles, of some of the greatest names in literature and in arms, and of not a few among the most intelligent and wealthy in the middle class, as giving to it their honest preference before all the systems of that age. The most interesting space, beyond all comparison, in the history of British intellect, was the space between 1640 and 1660; but the true manhood of those

lies the secret of the success and character of New England. Every child, as it was born into the world, was lifted from the earth by the genius of the country, and, in the statutes of the land, received as its birthright a pledge of the public care for its morals and its mind."

memorable times was clearly the manhood of English Independency. Many noble spirits then sighed to be free, — free in law, free in thought, free in utterance, — and it was in the nature of Independency to give them what they sought."[1] And what province, we may ask, without any boasting, has produced a larger number of the imperial minds of the present age, of those most distinguished for all that constitutes a complete and efficient manhood, than New England, where Congregationalism, more than anywhere else in the world, exerts its elevating influences alike upon all classes in society?

Carry, then, the church polity of the Pilgrims to the great West; carry it into all the borders of our country; carry it over the world. It is a fair argument for the great wisdom of this course, that the system itself is so divinely fitted to all classes in society, reaching the *masses* of the people, and elevating everywhere the popular mind and the popular character.

2. In the second place, the polity of the Pilgrims in the church is preëminently congenial with, and tends to promote, republicanism in the state. This form of church government is purely democratic. It intimates to the people their *right* to govern them-

[1] See Congregationalism and Modern Society, by Robert Vaughan, D. D., pp. 79, 80.

selves, and at the same time convinces them that self-government in the state, as well as in the church, is possible. It also tends to prepare them to use the rights and privileges secured in civil freedom, intelligently and properly; and so its whole influence and tendency, in this regard, is towards a democratic or republican form of civil government.[1]

This powerful tendency of Congregationalism has been frequently recognized as an historical fact. Even David Hume, speaking of the Puritans, whose ecclesiastical tendency was so obviously towards the freest church polity, was candid enough to affirm, that, "to this sect the English owe the whole freedom of their constitution." Lord Brougham affirms of the Independents, that they are "a body of men to be held in lasting veneration for the unshaken fortitude with which, in all times, they have maintained their attachment to civil liberty; men to whose ancestors England will ever acknowledge a boundless debt of gratitude, as long as freedom is prized among us. For, I freely confess it, they, with whatever ridicule some may visit their excesses, or with whatever blame others, they, with the zeal of martyrs and with the purity of the early Christians, the skill and courage of the most renowned warriors, achieved for England the free constitution

[1] See Appendix, note F.

which she now enjoys." Of the same character is the testimony of Lord King. "As for toleration," he says, "or any true notion of religious liberty, or any general freedom of conscience, we owe them not in the least degree to what is called the Church of England. On the contrary, we owe all these to the Independents in the time of the Commonwealth, and to Locke, their most enlightened and illustrious disciple." "We are prepared to expect," says a learned English author, "that those belonging to Independent churches, being accustomed to self-government, will sympathize in a liberal and popular form of civil administration where the people are fairly and fully represented. If they perceive that the interests of a spiritual society are best promoted by encouraging all the members to understand and feel their personal responsibility in the transaction of ecclesiastical business, they will be led to infer that the form of civil government which provides for a like sense of responsibility by allowing the people generally to exercise the rights of freemen, cannot be wrong. Habituated to self-government in the one department, they will desire the same principles in another. Such as live under the prelatic system, where the clergy are sent to them without their wishes being consulted or the nature of their wants studied, and where they are exempted, to a large extent, from the exercise of independent thought, will more readily acquiesce in a constitution under which they possess a like exemption. But men who are intrusted with a weighty commission in things spiritual will not be so easily satisfied with the passiveness of a condition where the few shut them out from the exercise of rights belonging to every subject of a free government. They will carry the same principles of liberty into the one department which they cherish in the other, believing them to be sanctioned of Heaven for the promotion, not less of the temporal than of the spiritual well-being of mankind." This natural and inevitable tendency of Congregationalism to promote civil and religious freedom is manifest throughout the entire history of this church order in England. The Independents never wavered in their demand for religious toleration, nor in their defence of it when obtained. It was by this persistent adherence to those principles of liberty taught them by their church polity that they saved England, not only from the tyranny to which prelacy always tends, but also from that with which even the Presbyterians sought to destroy her religious freedom the only time they were ever in power with the civil government. "Twice in their native land," history affirms, the Puritans "saved the British constitution from being crushed by the usurpations of the Stuarts." "Where," asks one of New England's greatest orators,[1] speaking of the Puritans, "where, in the long series of ages that furnish the matter of history, was there ever one [race], — *where one* better fitted, by the possession of the highest traits of man, to do the noblest work of man; better fitted to consummate and establish the Reformation, — to save the English constitution, at its last gasp, from the fate of other European constitutions, and prepare, on the granite and iced mountain summits of the New World, a still better rest for a still better liberty?"

But, not to speak further of Independency as the source and stay of English liberty, what is the relation of the free church polity of the Pilgrims to our own republicanism? We could not live under an absolute despotism. We love our civil freedom. It is our pride, and the hope of the world. But how came our government to be republican? The first settlers of this country did not come hither to establish this particular form of a government, or, indeed, any independent government whatever. They came hither from various motives; but this was not, to any general extent, one of them. And when, at last, the time came for them to renounce all kingly rule and to set up an independent civil organ-

[1] Hon. Rufus Choate.

ization, many opposed it as one of the worst calamities that could befall the country, while very many of those who approved of the Revolution, yet regretted that they should *be driven* to the measure. Our fathers, it is true, came hither for religious and civil freedom; but they had hoped to enjoy this without going to the full length of pure republicanism. How happened it, then, when an independent government came to be instituted, that it assumed this particular form? Doubtless many influences conspired to this result. But this question has not been duly weighed. The really determinative cause of our particular form of government has not been made sufficiently prominent. There is a connection between the church polity of the Pilgrim Fathers and the civil polity which they adopted, and also between their civil polity and that which the nation subsequently accepted, which has not been sufficiently traced and pondered. The purely democratic form of government in the Church at Leyden, already entrenched in the warm affections of the Pilgrims, led to the adoption of a corresponding form of civil government on board the Mayflower for the colony at Plymouth. It has been said, and it is true, that it was a *Congregational church meeting* that first suggested the idea of a New England town meeting; and a New England town meeting embodies all the germinal principles of our state and national governments.[1] Unquestionably, through

[1] "For more than eighteen years," says Mr. Bancroft, speaking of the Plymouth Colony, "'the whole body of the male inhabitants' constituted the legislature; the state was governed, like our towns, as a strict democracy; and the people were frequently convened to decide on executive, not less than on judicial, questions." Thus perfectly was the government of the state modelled after that of their church.

"The New Testament is emphatically a republican book. It sanctions no privileged orders; it gives no exclusive rights. All who imbibe its spirit and obey its precepts are recognized as equals, — children of the same Father, brethren and sisters in Christ, and heirs to a common inheritance. In the spirit of these kind and endearing relations, the first Christians formed themselves into little republican communities, acknowledging no head but Jesus Christ, and regulating all their concerns by mutual consultation, and a popular vote of the brotherhood. In these distinct and independent societies was realized, for the first time in this world, the perfect idea of civil and religious liberty. The Puritans imbibed the same spirit and derived their principles from the same pure source of light, of holiness and freedom. They modelled their churches after the primitive form, and founded them on the basis of entire independence and equality of rights. . . . . 'These were the men who settled New England. They came hither, bearing in their bosoms the sacred love of liberty and religion; and ere they left the little bark that had borne them across the ocean, they formed themselves 'into a civil body politic,' having for its basis this fundamental principle, that they *should be ruled by the majority*. Here is brought out

this channel came the strongest of the influences that conspired to make our form of civil government republican. For the members of the church at Plymouth influenced the churches at Salem, Boston, and Charlestown to adopt the same church polity with themselves; and thus was brought to bear upon the men of those places the same influence that had been so long moulding the political opinions of the members of the Leyden-Plymouth Church. And then, by the further extension of this church polity, with the gradual multiplication and growth of the colonies, this same influence was brought to bear upon all New England, and actually formed the political opinions of those of her leading men who were afterwards called to help construct our national government. It is very significant of the powerful working of this influence of Congregationalism upon the public mind immediately before the founding of the republic, that, in the single year 1772, the famous book, written by the Rev. John Wise more than half

the grand idea of a free, elective government. Here is the germ of that tree of liberty which now rears its lofty top to the heavens, spreading its branches over the length and breadth of our land, and under whose shade seventeen millions of freemen are reposing. The spirit of all our free civil and religious institutions was in the breasts of our Pilgrim fathers." — *Hawes' Tribute to the Memory of the Pilgrims*, as quoted by Dr. Coleman, in his Primitive Church, pp. 240, 241.

a century before, and entitled, "A Vindication of the Government of the Churches of New England," was reprinted *twice*, and the second reprint largely subscribed for by leading political men. In this book, two editions of which were thus scattered broadcast among the people only four years before the Declaration of Independence, and fifteen before the formation of the Constitution of the United States, thousands of the intelligent voters of New England read many a profound political truth, which must have stirred their souls with an unconquerable purpose to maintain their civil rights against all usurpation and tyranny. There is the true ring of our republican freedom in the following sentences, taken at random, from its pages: "*By a natural right, all men are born free;* and, nature having set all men upon a level and made them equals, no servitude or subjection can be conceived without inequality; and this cannot be made without usurpation or force in others, or voluntary compliance in those who resign their freedom, and give away their degree of natural being." "The first human subject and original of civil power is *the people.*" "The prince who strives to subvert the fundamental laws of the society is the traitor and the rebel, and not the people, who endeavor to preserve and defend their own." "A democracy was the noble government which beat out in all the bad weather of ten bloody persecutions under the management of antiquity." "The end of all good government is to cultivate humanity and promote the happiness of all, and the good of every man in all his rights, his life, liberty, estate, honor, etc., without injury or abuse done to any." It was a book with such sentiments as these that Congregationalism gave to New England at that critical juncture in her history when the people were preparing to decide upon the form of their national government. And this is only one of many similar indications of the powerful influence which our church polity was then exerting upon the people, and by which it was rapidly moulding their political opinions, and preparing them to constitute and maintain a strictly republican government. We are not at all surprised to find one of the delegates from Massachusetts to the Federal Convention a few years afterwards telling that body, with great emphasis, that "there was not a one thousandth part of his fellow-citizens who were not against every approach towards monarchy."

Nor was the influence of this church polity confined to New England. It reached some, at least, of those men beyond her borders who afterwards took a prominent part in laying the foundations of the republic. "Several years before the American Revolution, there was, near the house of Mr. Jefferson, in Virginia, a church which was governed on Congregational principles, and whose monthly meetings he often attended. Being asked how he was pleased with their church government, he replied that it had struck him with great force, and interested him very much ; that he considered it the only form of pure democracy that then existed in the world, and *had concluded* that it would be the best plan of government for the American colonies."[1] It is said to have been the opinion of Mr. Pitt, "that, if the Church of England had been efficiently established in the North American colonies, they would never have refused allegiance to the British crown." English statesmen early discerned, what many in our own country now fail to see, that Congregationalism, far more than any other church polity, cherishes republicanism in the state ; and it indicates the extent and the sincerity of their fears in this respect, that they "sent agents hither for the purpose of securing the abolition of our ecclesiastical polity, and introducing a more authoritative and ostentatious government."[2] It is, moreover, already the verdict of dispassionate history, that in the Mayflower came hither the germ of our republic. Mr. Bancroft

[1] See Jefferson's Notes on Virginia.

[2] See Sermon on Duties of New England Clergy, by Prof. E. A. Park, D. D., p. 15.

speaks of the civil compact formed by the Plymouth colony as "the birth of popular constitutional liberty." And again, speaking of the Pilgrims, he says: "The citizens of the United States should cherish the memory of those who founded a state on the basis of democratic liberty, — the fathers of the country, — the men who, as they first trod the soil of the New World, scattered the seminal principles of republican freedom and national independence." "To Congregationalism," says an eminent journalist,[1] "we doubtless owe the free and happy structure of our political institutions; for wherein they are not directly imitated from that excellent model, they were framed by those whose minds were deeply imbued with the spirit and liberality of its principles." There is — there must be — a connection between the government of the church and that of the state, not necessarily formal and coerced, but none the less mighty because it is simply a free, undesigned connection of silent and formative influence; and nowhere is that connection more obvious than between the church polity of the Pilgrims and the form of our civil government. Our fathers first learned that there could be a church without a bishop, and then they knew there could be a state without a king. In

[1] David Hale.

the brotherhood of the local church, in that pure democracy organized for the purpose of promoting personal holiness and the worship and service of God, was first caught the true idea of civil freedom, as founded upon the intelligence and virtue of the people. Our popular government lay in embryo on board the Mayflower, all-environed with its only possible preservatives, popular intelligence and popular virtue. The idea born there, and embodied in a civil constitution for that little democracy, grew with the growth of the colonies, gradually expelling from the thoughts and affections of the people all other theories of civil government, until finally it enthroned itself in the national mind, and then embodied itself in our national government.

Now it is a fair question, whether our form of government can be wholly, or even for the most part, dissevered from the church polity that begat it, and yet survive. The problem of our republicanism is yet to be solved; and who can say that that problem is not indissolubly linked with this other, whether that church polity of the Pilgrims which is related to our civil polity as a mother to her child is to be shut up in one corner of our country, as if it were some monster, that, if unloosed, would devour her own offspring, or is to go unimpeded into all parts of the land, and everywhere, by its silent but mighty educating influences, elevate the masses of the people, and render them competent to be citizens of a free government. One thing, at least, we may affirm: Let the church polity of the Pilgrims have free sway in all the borders of our country, and the perpetuity of those free institutions which it has brought into existence and nurtured to maturity, and with which its whole spirit is so singularly congenial, would be in far less danger than now.[1] Here

[1] "There is nothing that so arouses the activity of the intellect, — nothing reaches down so far into the very elements of our being, as the conviction of our personal duty in conducting the affairs of the kingdom of God on earth. The obligation to select wise legislators in the state, to secure the passage of wholesome laws, invigorates the mind less, expands the charities of the heart less, than the obligation to watch over, to advise, and to aid, the assembly of the brethren. If the pious men in the provinces of France had been trained, during the last two centuries, under the discipline of New England churches, judging for themselves with regard to doctrine and practice, feeling themselves called of Heaven to give their individual advice or their own individual reasons, at the assembling of the local church, and at the ecclesiastical council, there would have gone forth from these men an influence quickening the mind of the entire community, and the nation, which is now too ill trained for preserving a republic, would have been too well trained to endure an usurpation. And it is partly for the maintaining of our political institutions, for the educating of our people to give an intelligent suffrage, that we desire to see the same ecclesiastical

lies one great argument for a more general and rapid extension of the Congregational church polity. It is to save our country. It is to infuse into our national life its only preservative and vitalizing element. It is to carry into every part of the land that one instrumentality which, above all others, is fitted to prepare the people, by nurturing their intelligence and virtue, to appreciate and maintain a free government. By all the fond hopes, therefore, which you entertain for the future of your country under its popular institutions, carry the ecclesiastical principles of the Pilgrims into every part of the land, and let them work; let them *inform* the popular mind; let them educate the people to give a wise suffrage, and, by a thousand silent influences, render them generally competent to appreciate and perpetuate the rich civil heritage they have received from the Pilgrim Fathers.

3. In the third place, the church polity of the Pilgrims has peculiar fitnesses to the present imperfect state of the members of a Christian church. There doubtless are, and, in the present order of things,

principles moulding the character of our Western States as helped to form the intellect and conscience of our New England colonies." — *See Address before the American Congregational Union*, by Prof. E. A. Park, D. D., p. 23.

there doubtless must be, in every church, those who are not true Christians; while the best are but partially sanctified. The most perfect system of church government, in the hands of such men, will be worked more or less imperfectly. Out of such a state of the church, evils will arise, which no kind of church polity can wholly prevent. There will be wicked men to vex the church; there will be ambitious men seeking to make it a means of personal aggrandizement; there will be worldly men to kill out its very life by their spiritual deadness; there will be collisions of opinion and personal interest, animosities and heart-burnings between imperfect brethren, which will often embroil the whole church, and sometimes leave it in dissevered fragments. But we confidently affirm, that there is no system of church government that can so effectually restrain these evils, or, if they are not wholly restrained, can manage them with so little commotion in the world, and with so little injury to the church, as that of Congregationalism. There is little about this system that can be made to subserve the interests of wicked men. Its very simplicity is its protection from their wiles. It has no places of preferment, no ecclesiastical offices, towering high above all the churches, to tempt the ambition and employ the thoughts of ministers, when they should be caring for the flocks over which alone God has made them overseers. It has no ecclesiastical machinery raised above and controlling all the churches, of which wicked men, and even too aspiring good men, will always love to get the management, merely for the pleasure of working it, if not for more selfish purposes.[1] It has no rising grade of imposing judicatories, occasioning, in their management, endless collisions and wranglings and heart-burnings, employing themselves often year after year in hot debate over some trivial case of difficulty that would have been settled at one session of a local church, when its authority is understood to be supreme, and thus occupying a large portion of the invaluable time and strength of ministers, to the neglect of the great work of the gospel ministry. Still, difficulties will arise, even in complete, local churches; but, as these bodies are distinct, and independent of each

[1] "Who does not know that the curse of a graceless ministry has ever rested upon the church, to a greater or less extent, wherever they have not enjoyed the right of electing their own pastors? The rich and quiet livings of an establishment, especially if coupled with the authority, the distinction, and emoluments, of the Episcopal office, will ever be an object of ambition to worldly men. 'Make me a bishop,' — said an ancient idolator, — 'make me a bishop, and I will surely be a Christian.'" — *See The Primitive Church*, by Dr. Coleman, p. 84.

other, none can be injured except the one in which the difficulty happens to occur. And even in this the heat more generally soon effervesces, and leaves the waters as peaceful as before. As the local church is all open above, the steam that is generated in these embroilments passes quietly away, and does no harm; but where there is a great and compact system of machinery to gather and condense it, the greatest commotion, and wide spread disasters, often follow. In these consolidated systems of church government, the smallest difficulty in one church may, and often does, rend asunder a whole communion; while difficulties arising in the supreme government itself are almost sure to produce disastrous and irremediable divisions. Thus the Presbyterian Church in Scotland has already been rent into no less than five distinct fragments. The Presbyterian church of our own country is not an exception to this inevitable working of its system. These complicated, centralized church organizations are not the best fitted to secure the ends of a church in a world like ours. By their very structure they are too much exposed. In the great conflict with sin, they work to the greatest disadvantage, and often are only themselves shattered to pieces in their first encounter. But when the churches are all distinct and independent, connected only by the mutual attraction of

Christian love, there is no such exposure. Their working is then like that of the planetary system, where each world is united to all the rest by the mutual attraction of gravitation, and where all collision is avoided by that simple centrifugal force that keeps each world moving on in its own course, intent only upon its own business. And if by chance any disaster should happen to one of these planets, — as perhaps there once did, — and it should be shattered into a thousand fragments, still all the rest would move on in their wonted harmony. But suppose our planetary system was less divine, and more human, — suppose the worlds, instead of rolling on in their present easy and graceful independence, were all connected by some vast system of machinery reared above them and resting on them, having all the weight and rigidity of bars of iron, and so stiffening the whole system into one great and imposing body, — who cannot see, that then the slightest shock upon one world would be equally a shock to all, and that the ruin of one might be the ruin of the whole? Who cannot see also, that all the grating and jarring of the superincumbent machinery would be felt in threatening vibrations alike by every world? and that, if any great disaster should happen to this machinery in the process of its working, it would be equally a disaster to all the worlds which it embraced and connected? The divine method in the planetary system is better. And, for the same reason, we say that the divine method of connecting the churches of Christ is better than any consolidating system. Let them be, as the Saviour and the apostles left them, free, local churches, each distinct and complete in itself, moving on easily and gracefully in its own line of duty, and yet all united by Christian love, and ever ready for the interchange of kind offices.

But it is sometimes objected to this Congregational system, that it fosters too much life in the individual churches; that it does not keep them all quiet and tractable; that it makes the members feel their independence too much; and so stimulates them to intemperate zeal and action, making the churches so many hotbeds of error and fanaticism.[1] But the ground of this inconsiderate objection we regard as one of the greatest excellences of the system. The superabundant light and heat of the sun are great blessings, though they may produce some unnecessary and even noisome vegetation, and now and then momentarily fill the air with troublesome exhalations. We glory in just this feature of our church polity. We believe that life is better

[1] See Appendix, Note G.

than death ; — that some unnecessary commotion or visionary action is not so great an evil as utter stagnation. Existence, to a man who is always asleep, is not preferable to death. "Aloof from practice," says Sir William Hamilton, "a waking error is better than the sleeping truth." The church of Christ *should* be a region of the intensest action. It is placed in a world that is all glowing and surging with life, and God never designed that his church should be like an island of ice on a sea of fire. The intensity of its burning zeal for God should even surpass the intensest ardor with which the world around it is pervaded. Too much life in a church of Christ! Impossible. Indeed, we know not what would become of some of our more staid evangelical denominations, were they not constantly receiving the overflow of this very life, and thus replenishing both their wasting ministry and membership with men converted to God amidst this same intense action in our Congregational churches. It is right to look at facts, and guide ourselves by them ; and we are convinced, that, could accurate statistics be gathered, showing the extent to which several other denominations are dependent, upon Congregationalism for both ministers and laymen, it would not only surprise the world, but would be one of the strongest arguments for our system, and one of the strongest, too, with which I could urge you to-day to carry this elevating and energizing church polity into every part of our country.[1] Give

[1] "Proclamation has been made in high places, that within the last thirty years, 'about *three hundred* clergymen and licentiates of other denominations have sought the ministerial commission from the hands of' bishops [in the Episcopal church]; that *two thirds* of all 'the present clergy of the church have come from other folds,' and that of *two hundred and eighty-five* persons ordained by a single bishop in New England, *two hundred and seven* were converts from other denominations. If the triumph were, that these hundreds of clergymen and thousands of laymen had been transformed from sin to holiness, we would exult in the glad news. We call heaven and earth to witness, that we rejoice in the advance of any sect whose pure aim is to gather the wanderers from virtue into the congregation of the saints. But no; the boast is, that converts have been made not from iniquity to godliness, but from sects and denominations to what is called, in a peculiar style of catholicism, *the* church." — *Sermon on the Duties of the New England Clergy*, by Prof. E. A. Park, D. D., pp. 44, 45.

There can be no doubt of the fact, that the Episcopalian church of New England is dependent, in the largest degree, upon Congregationalism for nominally converted laymen and clergymen. The fact is remarkably significant of the comparative evangelical efficiency of the two systems. And yet the unblushing manner in which Episcopalians often seek to proselyte members of Congregational churches, at the same time that they condemn their church polity, is peculiarly instructive with regard to the capabilities of human nature. When they seek to

this divine model of a living church to the West; give it to the North and to the South; and let its

convert men to Christ, rather than to proselyte them to their church, we do not complain; we will pray for their success. But "already have some of our laymen been told that their pastor was never really ordained." "Our candidates for the ministry have been pointed to the bishops' robes, that float before the fancy of young men." "Our ordained clergymen have been approached with assurances that rich preferments awaited them if they would cast contempt on their ordination, and kneel down in worship. 'Come unto us,' has been the language addressed to one; 'for we have peace within the church, but all is division out of it.' 'Come unto us,' has been the language addressed to a second; 'for we need your aid in quieting our dissensions.' 'Come unto us,' has been the language to a third; 'for the church has a beautiful unity.' 'Come unto us,' has been the language to a fourth; 'for the church is made the more interesting by the varieties which are embraced in it.' 'Come unto us,' has been said here; 'for we have a creed which prevents all such discussions as will always prevail among dissenters.' 'Come unto us,' has been said there; 'for we always insure the greatest freedom of thought and debate.' 'Come unto us,' has been whispered in this place; 'for the church is truly and securely evangelical.' 'Come unto us,' has been intimated in that place; 'for we stand in perishing need of evangelical men, who may save us from the reign of fashion and vanity.' 'Come unto us,' has been the invitation to a pastor who had been ordained without a display of apostolical succession; 'for although you have been often ejected from your pulpits heretofore, we will give you a staff of office which no popular

life overflow. Let it give converted men to all other denominations until they are full; yea, let it give them to all the world with a lavish hand, in beautiful imitation of its great Author, who, in the overflow of his infinite love, rains his blessings on both the just and the unjust.

4. In the fourth place, the church polity of the Pilgrims is peculiarly fitted to prepare the church to grapple successfully with the organic sins and general wickedness of the world. We have reason to believe, both from the divinity of this system and from facts in its history, that in no other form of a church can Christianity be made so effective in its great work of renovating the world. From its very structure, its aggressive power is superior to that of any other ecclesiastical system. As it calls all the

majority shall take away; we will save you from exhausting labors; we will furnish you with prayers already made, and will allow your sermons to be few and short and inoffensive.' 'Come unto us,' has been the inviting offer to a missionary; 'for we need your services in awakening among our clergy the spirit of missions, and we can write your name, and give you a title, among the patriarchs of the East.'" — Prof. E. A. Park's Sermon on the Duties of the New England Clergy, pp. 43, 44.

It is also a well-known fact, that, besides the Episcopalian church, the Methodist and New School Presbyterian churches are largely indebted to Congregationalism for both church-members and ministers.

members of the church into personal action, it increases the aggregate effective force. This church polity is consistent with the scriptural teaching, that *every* disciple of Jesus is a soldier under the Captain of his Salvation, for it marshals every church-member to the conflict. Like its great Author, it says to the timid and the faltering, "Whosoever will save his life shall lose it; but whosoever shall lose his life for my sake and the gospel, the same shall save it." As it places upon every member alike the fearful responsibility of the watch and care of the church, so it tends to make them all alike regard themselves responsible for the general interests of the kingdom of Christ in the world.

It is thus we account for the spontaneous and large liberality of Congregational churches in founding academies, colleges, and schools of divinity, and in starting and carrying forward so many magnificent schemes for the evangelization of the world. It is a significant fact, that all, or nearly all, of the great national benevolent societies of our land, which are doing so much to give tracts and Bibles and Sabbath schools and ministers and missionaries to the world, had their origin in Congregational churches, and, for the most part, have since been sustained by them. The men who have been most efficient in devising large things for the kingdom of Christ without reference to their own sect or to any sect, during the last half century, have been themselves Congregationalists, and have relied mainly upon Congregational churches for aid to carry out their generous plans. "The same divine,"[1] it is said, "who was one of the most active in originating the oldest theological seminary in the land, was also one of the most active in starting the associated effort for our domestic missions, and was one of the two men who projected the oldest board for foreign missions; the cause of learning, and the cause of an aggressive Christianity, being identified in his esteem. Two of the same divines[2] who originated that ancient seminary were the first to propose our most ancient education society, and one of the most honored pupils of that seminary,[3] stated, a few months before his demise: "I could never have done what I did in the incipient movements of the American Tract Society, nor in the forming of the American Temperance Society, nor in the establishment of the American Sabbath Union, unless I had enjoyed the aid of a popular and unfettered church government, allowing me to combine the

[1] Dr. Samuel Spring.

[2] Drs. Pearson and Morse.

[3] Dr. Justin Edwards.

agencies of enterprising individuals, whenever and wherever I could find them, — men accustomed to act for themselves, — minute-men, ready for every good work, without waiting for the jarring and warring of church courts."[1] The first organized Christian effort in the world in behalf of seamen was made in Boston under the influence of Congregationalism. Through these numerous reformative and missionary movements, in which the members of the churches have been brought to grapple hand to hand with various forms of sin without any intervening and cumberous ecclesiastical machinery, Christianity has been made to assert something of its primitive aggressive power. It is an undeniable fact, that, since the revival of Congregationalism within the last century or two, a wonderful missionary spirit has been awakened among the disciples of Christ,[2] and the gospel has advanced more rapidly and farther over the world than during all the intervening centuries since the corruption of

[1] Address before the American Congregational Union, May, 1854, by Prof. E. A. Park, D. D., p. 45.

[2] "It will be acknowledged," says an Episcopalian writer, "that the strength of our brethren, [referring to his brethren of other denominations,] in their missionary operations, lies in New England, and among the descendants of the Puritans." — Tract upon the Position of the Protestant Episcopal Church, p. 14.

the apostolic and primitive form of a church. In the first age of Christianity, when this church polity had full sway, the missionary spirit rose high, and the gospel spread rapidly over the world; and now when this church polity is again revived, this same missionary spirit is again awakened, and once more we see the churches engaged in obeying the Redeemer's last great command.

But this is not the only proof of the singular fitness of this system for powerful aggressive action. There are certain great evils and sins in the world, with which the church is constantly coming into conflict; and when brought to the encounter, there are but two courses before her; she must either take her stand before them and resist them even unto death, if need be, or bend, compromise with them, and so receive on her own fair forehead the foul stain of their guilt. There are such sins; prevalent sins; fashionable sins; systematized sins; interwoven often into the very texture of society, into the very fabric of civil government. Now if, in the providence of God, a church of Christ is placed in such a relation to these sins that she must either give her consent and sanction to them, or reprobate and resist them, nothing can be plainer than her duty. She must wash her hands of those sins, whatever they are, and at all costs. And it is in just such an emergency as this, that those Christians who have adopted the church polity of the Pilgrims are most likely and most prompt to do their duty. Not only has the previous training of the men under the system prepared them to act independently and manfully in such a case, but they have comparatively little temptation to swerve from the right. There is nothing about their church organization that will be put in jeopardy by the encounter. They are all free, and ready for duty. Had they a vast and complicated ecclesiastical machinery uniting the churches of their communion, with which the sin had become all intertwined, they might say, "If we touch the sin, we shall rend the church;" and so, to save their ecclesiastical system, they would nourish the sin. But, as members of distinct, local churches, they have no ecclesiastical organization whose interests they must so carefully consult, before they can obey God. They have no such incumbrance weighing them down when their heavenly Master is calling them to action. They can be influenced by no fear either that their course will be reviewed by some high church judicatory, which may already have become compromised with the sin, and virtually pledged to its support. They have nothing above them but conscience and God; and when these are calling them to duty, their church polity leaves them perfectly free to obey. The independent local church never feels the influence of a mighty, overshadowing church power breathing down upon it, and stiffening all its members so that they dare not stir for very fear. You do not hear them constantly and servilely appealing to *the book*, *the book*, and to the authoritative decisions of high ecclesiastical judicatories; nor, in any great question of Christian duty, inquiring, first of all, for the limits of their *constitutional* power! The Bible is the only book which they honor with the distinctive appellation, *The Book.* The Scriptures are their only and sufficient rule of Christian faith and practice, and the authority of Christ is alone above that of their local church. Consequently, they are never cowed down into a cringing attitude by an imposing ecclesiastical organism. They are never cramped by formality or fear, or any of the rigidities of a complicated and centralizing church system. When called to decide upon a course of action, they can consult conscience and the Bible without once thinking of their church organization. And in this is disclosed one of the greatest excellences of our ecclesiastical polity. It accomplishes its own work quietly and efficiently, securing to us all the ends of a church, and yet never interposes between us and our duty.

It has no influences to foster that sectarian spirit that leads one to think more of his church than of duty or of Christ.

Nor is this all the proof of the great aggressive power of this divine church polity. It is, from its very nature, one of the greatest foes on earth to all great systematized or legalized sins. Tyrants hate it. All forms of despotism and oppression gnash their teeth upon it. Take some of its primary principles, and apply them to any system of wickedness, and contemplate the result. Take, for instance, its law of discipline, — that simple but imperative law that is virtually discarded by other church polities. That law of our Saviour, without any sycophancy or apology, places all the members of the church upon the same level, — Greek and barbarian, bond and free, master and slave, — and makes them all kings and priests unto God. Look at the following application, which has been aptly made of it to the sin of human bondage. "It says to the slave, who has been refashioned in his Sovereign's image: If thy brother, who claims the ownership of thee, shall trespass against thee, go and tell him his fault, between thee and him alone; if he shall hear thee, thou hast gained thy brother; but if he will not hear thee, then take with thee one or two more of thy fellow bondmen; and if he shall neglect to hear them, tell his fault to the church, even if they be all his legal property; and if he neglect to hear *that* church, let him be unto thee as an heathen man, and whatsoever ye shall bind on earth shall be bound in heaven.[1] Why has not this scriptural church polity gone into every portion of our country? Why is it so much dreaded, and so repeatedly and earnestly affirmed to be a good system for New England, but not for any other part of the land? Why is it so violently maligned the moment it is seen crossing the boundary line of the Eastern States and approaching the "peculiar institutions" of some other States? One reason is obvious. No scheme of despotism, however strongly barricaded by legal enactments, can stand before it. It cuts right through our American system of human oppression, and levels it to the ground. At one fell sweep it places master and slave side by side, brothers in Christ, with the rights of brothers; and, that done, slavery is no more. This systematized sin is our country's great and growing peril. Developing itself by inherent laws in the stern march of history slowly yet inevitably as it does, it some-

[1] Address before the American Congregational Union, May, 1854, by E. A. Park, D. D.

times seems as if our free institutions were already doomed. Do we love our country? Then confront this gigantic evil with its true antagonism. Carry out into the land, far beyond the borders of New England, that divine church polity, which, above all others, is fitted to grapple successfully with this and every such monster evil."

5. In the fifth place, the church polity of the Pilgrims is peculiarly fitted to promote the spirituality of Christians. It promotes it in all those ways in which, as we have seen, it calls them into personal and responsible action. It cherishes it, not only by this vigorous exercise of it, but also by habituating each church-member to stand face to face before his God, without any intervening ecclesiasticism; by intrusting all the members alike with the watch and care of souls, and holding them accountable only to Christ. The pressure of such personal responsibilities is eminently fitted to lead men to prayer, and a closer walk with God. The fact that Christ is understood to be the only head of even a local church tends to bring the members at once into intimate communion with him. The close affinity of this church polity with the deepest and truest piety is likewise clearly indicated by the fact, that in the great religious reformations that have occurred in the history of the church, there

has usually been plainly discernible a strong tendency towards this system, if not an actual adoption of it. Luther himself was at first a Congregationalist, but afterwards gave up the system from fear that all "the poor people" were not well enough trained for it. He should have let the system itself have trained the people. This church polity is like a plant, that always enriches its own soil. Had the great reformer but persevered for a short time in the experiment, he would have remained a Congregationalist. Even in Calvin and Knox there can be discerned, at least, a tendency towards this form of a church. They both advised measures to bring the *members* of the church into *responsible action* as a means of their spiritual improvement. The close affinity of this system with the spirit of missions has already been noticed. It quickens the Christian's sympathy with his Redeemer. It cherishes the love of souls. One of the leading objects of the Pilgrims in coming to this country was to convert the heathen to Christ; and from the days of Eliot to our own, Congregationalism has ever been foremost in the sacred work of missions. The tendency of this form of a church to promote the spirituality of its members is also strikingly illustrated by its natural alliance with revivals of religion. New England, the great seat of Congregationalism, has been emphatically the land of revivals. And wherever this divine ecclesiastical polity has been adopted, it has shown a strong tendency to put to rout all formality and spiritual deadness, and bring men into spiritual life.

Now it is this church polity, with all these its undeniable excellences; its peculiar fitness to elevate the masses of the people, and thus prepare them for the freest, highest form of civil government; its surpassing adaptedness to the present state of the church and the world, working with the least possible friction, and yet with the greatest efficiency; simple, quiet, unostentatious in itself, and yet terrible in its aggressive action; at the same time having the closest affinity with the deepest, truest piety; — it is this *living*, *divine* church; the single, local church of the Pilgrims; the church of Christ and the apostles; with all its unquestionable and preëminent excellences, that I ask you to-day to give to your country. I confidently believe, that ultimately, in the history of this world's redemption, this form of a church will become universally prevalent. By its origin, its nature, and facts in its history already attesting its marvellous capabilities, I am fully persuaded that it is the only form of a church in which Christianity can displace sectarianism, triumph over every sin, and so bring on the world's complete evangelization. All hail to the coming time in our own country, when the mighty power of this simple but divine system shall be working in all the borders of our land; in the east and in the west, in the north and in the south; sending out into the community a thousand quickening influences; grappling fearlessly with all the sins of the land, and holding on in the struggle until the people shout the pæan of her victory! All hail to that yet further future in the world, when the disciples of one Lord shall no longer be divided up into warring sects, fenced around with high, frowning, denominational walls; when we shall no more hear of the Congregational Church, the Presbyterian Church, the Episcopal Church, the Methodist Church, the Baptist Church, but when all shall be simple, local churches, each distinct and complete in itself, all standing upon the same broad level of belief and fellowship, — one Lord, one faith, one baptism! All hail to that glorious future, the world's millennium!

APPENDIX.

NOTE A.

Many Congregational ministers in New England, during the last quarter of a century, have never for once advocated their own church polity in their public ministrations; and some few there are, indeed, who, when they have made any reference to the subject either in preaching or in writing, have done so in a half apologetic strain, and have been especially particular to deprecate all earnest advocacy of Congregationalism as of divine authority. Take the following as a fair illustration: "With regard to the appointment of any special form of church government, it would seem that there is a wise silence in the New Testament. The genius of Christianity forbids an adherence to any form of ecclesiastical order as essential to the existence of a church of Christ. Our preference for the Congregational form of church government is not properly founded on any prescriptions in the New Testament, but on our convictions that this form is most accordant with the genius of Christianity and of republican institutions. But so surely as we insist on Congregationalism as having any 'divine right' or authority, and we seek to propagate Congregationalism with such convictions, we are as surely High-

Churchmen and Puseyites as can anywhere be found. At the same time we may believe that the Congregational form of government is nearer to the spirit of the New Testament than any other." The position assumed here is, that Christ and the apostles left to Christians no specific form of church government, and that therefore no one form, properly speaking, is any more *scriptural* than any other. Popery, Episcopacy, Methodism, Presbyterianism, as systems of church government, are as truly of *divine* authority as Congregationalism; that is, no system can be defended on this ground. Congregationalism, then, if advocated at all, must be advocated not on the ground of its being scriptural or of divine authority, but on the ground of expediency.

This is the Erastian view. It is the position frequently assumed by the advocates of centralized systems of church government. They adopt this as an easy mode of getting rid of the scriptural argument, of which they are aware they can make nothing in their favor, and of clearing the way for a most strenuous defence of their own systems on other than scriptural grounds. But when a *Congregationalist* assumes this position, it will generally be found, as a matter of fact, that he does it, not to prepare the way for the defence of his own ecclesiastical polity, but rather as an apology for holding to it loosely, and for being ready, at any moment when circumstances may require it, to surrender it for some other system.

It is instructive to compare this modern style of remarking upon Congregationalism, an example of which is given above, with the manner of discourse upon this subject formerly in vogue among Congregational ministers. It shows what a change has taken place in this regard, and how insipid such a belief, and such a strain of remark upon our church polity, are, in comparison with the manly faith and practice of the New England fathers, and of the English advocates of our church polity. Let any one read the above denial that Congregationalism has any divine right or scriptural authority, and then turn to John Cotton and hear him say of this same church polity, that "it was instituted and practised in the first ages of Christianity, and our Saviour himself is the true author of this first ecclesiastical state of the church;" or to Cotton Mather, and hear him affirm that "we have a platform left us that is according to the word of our gracious Lord;" or to the pages of John Robinson, and see how he "vindicated, cleared, and defended it, on *scriptural* grounds, and by victorious argument," and he will be convinced that a great change, in this respect, has gradually come over the ministry of our denomination. John Owen, advocating the divine authority of Congregationalism, says that "Christ alone is the author, institutor, and appointer, in a way of authority and legislation, of the gospel church-state, its order, rule, and worship with all things constantly and perpetually belonging thereunto, or necessary to be observed therein. What is not so is of men, and not from heaven."[1] This same divine has one chapter with the caption, "Congregational churches alone suited unto the ends of Christ in the institution of his church;" and another with the caption, "No other church-state of divine institution." The famous book of John Wise, which is the legal accredited exposition of the Cambridge platform, makes no apology for defending Congregationalism on the ground of its divine authority, as well as on that of its conformity to "the light of nature." The Congregationalists of that day in New England did not hesitate to advocate their own church polity boldly and earnestly even in opposition to Presbyterianism. "An aristocracy,"

[1] Owen's Works, Vol. XV. p. 244.

says John Wise, "is a dangerous constitution in the church of Christ; as it possesses the presbytery of all church power. What has been observed sufficiently evinces it. And not only so, but from the nature of the constitution, for it has no more barrier to it against the ambition, insults, and arbitrary measures of men, than an absolute monarchy."[1] President Oakes, the fourth president of Harvard College, in an election sermon, as quoted by John Wise, says: "I profess that I look upon the discovery and settlement of the Congregational way, as the boon, the gratuity, the largeness, of divine bounty, which the Lord graciously bestowed on this people, that followed him into this wilderness, and who were separated from their brethren. Those good people who came over had more love, zeal, and affectionate desire of communion with God, in pure worship and ordinances, and did more in order to it, than others; and the Lord did more for them than for any people in the world, in showing them the pattern of his house, and the truer scriptural way of church government and administrations. God was certainly in a more than ordinary way present with his servants, in laying of our foundations; and in settling church order, according to the will and appointment of Christ. Consider what will be the sad issue of revolting from the way fixed on to one extreme or to another, whether it be to Presbyterianism or to Brownism."[2]

Nor has such an outspoken and manly advocacy of the church polity of the apostles and primitive Christians ceased to be heard in the pulpits of New England until within a comparatively few years. As late as the time of Dr. Emmons, we have an example of the defence of Con-

1 Vindication of the Government of New England Churches, p. 39.
2 Vindication of the Government of New England Churches, p. 19.

gregationalism that would have sounded familiar to the people of earlier New England history. "Every mode of church government," says Dr. Emmons, "is destructive of the rights and liberties of every Christian church except strict Congregationalism. Presbyterianism is destructive of the independence of every Christian church, and robs it of all the power and authority which Christ has given it. No Presbyterian church has a right to invite a candidate to preach among them, without the consent of the presbytery. And after they have invited him and are willing to settle him, they cannot get him ordained without the consent of the presbytery. And if he should be corrupt in sentiment or practice, they could not discipline him according to the steps that Christ has pointed out. He would first appeal to the presbytery, and if they should condemn him, he would appeal to the synod; and if they should condemn him, he could appeal to the general assembly, which might be hundreds of miles from his people; and if they should justify him, his people could have no relief. It is easy to see that this mode of church government is destructive to the rights of any particular church. So is Episcopalianism. An Episcopalian church has no independence; the government of it is in the hands of archbishops, bishops, and other inferior clergy. You know that all the Protestant world have loudly complained, and justly, of the ecclesiastical tyranny of the church of Rome, which has destroyed the independence of all the churches of the popish religion. Every mode of church government except strict Congregationalism is hostile to that perfect platform of church government which Christ has given us in the eighteenth of Matthew, and is more or less tyrannical. These human hierarchies, which have been the source of immense evils in the Christian world, ought to be destroyed; and they will undoubtedly be destroyed in the time of the millennium.

They are the bulwarks of error, delusion, and every species of moral corruption, and must be purged out of the Christian world before the church can become universally pure, and flourish. We have long been praying for the downfall of unchristian power and tyranny in the church of Rome; and we ought to pray for the downfall of every degree of that unchristian power in every other church in the world."

. . . .

. . . And now please to remember, that your peace, purity, and edification unitedly bind you, *to stand fast in the liberty wherewith Christ has made you free;* and maintain your original Congregational principles in opposition to every other mode of church government; and especially against Presbyterianism, which so many ministers throughout the United States are so zealously engaged to promote. If they should tell you that Christ has not instituted any particular form of church government, refer them to the eighteenth of Matthew, which ought to silence them. But if they deny that any platform of government is there instituted, ask them to show you the passage or the passages in the New Testament in which Christians are required to exercise any kind of ecclesiastical authority or discipline over one another. No man can tell. All who depart from Christ's platform of church government make one of their own, which must be unscriptural, unreasonable, and tyrannical. This has been, for ages, confirmed by all the persecutions to which Christians have been subjected. All persecutions have originated from ecclesiastical tyranny. But it is impossible for persecution to arise in strictly Congregational churches. They inflict no civil penalties on delinquents. Their discipline terminates in excommunication. Maintain Congregational discipline, and you are safe, but not otherwise." [1]

[1] Emmons's Works, Vol. V. pp. 455, 457.

It is very obvious, that if this nation is ever to inherit to any great degree the noble character and principles of the Pilgrims, Congregationalists must cease apologizing for the church polity of those godly men. If Christianity, disenthralled from human forms and inventions, is ever to exert its primitive power upon this great people, developing and perpetuating institutions more congenial with itself, and more mighty in their ennobling influences than the world has yet seen, Congregational ministers must cease begging pardon of their hearers and the world for having adopted the church polity of the apostles and the primitive Christians. At the present time there are unmistakable indications of a rapid return to the practice of the New England fathers in a bold and uncompromising defence of Congregationalism, not in a sectarian spirit, we trust, but from true love to Christ, and to the only form of a church which he has left to his people. To every thoughtful mind this change is one of the most marked features of the age, and one of the most hopeful for the maintenance of a pure and unfettered Christianity, and for the perpetuity of our civil institutions. The following is an illustration of the style of thought that is now becoming current in our denomination: —

"Are we to expect the perpetuity of centralization as an element of Protestantism? Why should we expect it? Protestantism has indeed made the Bible free, and left every Christian free to interpret it. But on which page of the Bible is there the remotest hint of a centralized church government, whether of the Presbyterian or Episcopal form? As we have already said, the Bible affords no evidence that such a conception had entered any man's mind in the apostolic age. How then does a free Bible tend to promote church centralization? On the contrary, it presents us the church under apostolic guidance, with no trace of centralization upon it.

"Is it said the experience of the church has demonstrated the necessity of such centralization beyond reasonable doubt or controversy? Where is that demonstration? In what ages of church history has it been wrought out? Was it in the Ancient Church, when each step towards centralization was a step towards the apostasy? Was it in the mediæval Church, when centralized church power wore out the patience of the saints for a thousand years? Or has this demonstration been wrought out since the Reformation, during which period, it is obvious, to any thoughtful reader of history, that centralized church government exists not from any past or present experience of its necessity, but as the embodiment of an idea derived from the past, and tenaciously cherished as sacred? And if experience has furnished any proof of its necessity or utility, it is in the working of the very ecclesiastical systems which we now see around us. And in order to succeed in the argument, the advocates of centralization must address themselves to a comparison of the results of their several systems with those of the localism of the apostolic age, of English and Scotch Independency, and of our own New England churches. We shall not shrink from any conclusions to which such an investigation will be likely to conduct."

. . . .

"We may argue as we please for the beneficial influence of sects, their obvious blighting and blasting effects are filling the hearts of thousands of the most devout and pious Christians with unutterable sorrow. And it is a sorrow which springs up from the deepest fountains of Christian love, and which no argument, however ingenious, can comfort. We even deny that the amount of effort and individual self-sacrifice for objects nominally religious are at all increased by the existence of sects. Where in this land will you find a liberality to the cause of missions equalling that of the New England churches to the American Foreign and Home Missionary Societies? And yet it is certain, that these contributions are not stimulated by denominational zeal. They are the product of no spirit of mere denominational propagandism.

"The foundations and endowments of the New England colleges have not come from denominational zeal; and he sadly misunderstands New England who supposes that they have. And yet, where else on our continent hath an equal liberality to the cause of learning been displayed? Indeed, he seems to us beside himself who imagines, that had New England presented throughout her history the same aspect of denominationalism which our country as a whole now presents, her efficiency in promoting religious interests would not have been greatly less than it has been.

"We are ready, therefore, to declare our conviction, ... that this conflict of sects, each aiming to extend its jurisdiction over the greatest possible numbers, and soliciting the allegiance of the same individuals, like all other conflicts, is a state of transition, and not of rest; and, therefore, in the nature of things, is transient, and while it lasts is fatally contradictory to that unity of his disciples for which our Lord prayed, and for which every Christian in every age must pray. We are persuaded that the 'sect system' is not the ultimate destiny of Protestantism in a country where it enjoys freedom of development.

"We believe, therefore, that the independence of the local church is the result towards which the principles of the Reformation steadily tend, and in which the church, disenthralled from all the forms and modifications of centralized church power, will at last find rest; in doctrine, purely and simply evangelical; in government, local, and recognizing the full equality of the Christian brotherhood; in ceremonies, receiving none but those appointed in the Divine Word, and granting all that liberty of opinion in respect to these which experience has shown to be necessary to accommodate the diversities of judgment likely to arise among Christian men honestly endeavoring to interpret the Sacred Oracles.

"For such a system we claim that it is but a reproduction of the church order of the apostles, which was in a great measure lost in the great antichristian apostasy; that while it gives opportunity for the full development of individual activity and efficiency, it more successfully provides than any other system has ever done for the great social wants of the church of Christ, so that its efficacy in perpetuating the gospel at home by permanent institutions, and sending it abroad by a world-wide spirit of missions, is greater than that of any other ecclesiastical system which has existed since the apostolic age."[1]

It is a cheering fact, that such sentiments as these now meet with a ready response from the hearts of increasing multitudes in our country. They have been, and are destined to be, the sentiments of the most thoughtful, the holiest, and the most unsectarian, of men. There is getting to be too much light abroad upon this subject for any recreant son of the Pilgrims safely to denounce those holy, self-denying fathers of New England as "High-Churchmen and Puseyites," because they defended their church polity "with victorious argument," on the ground of its scripturalness and divine authority.

NOTE B.

The original word, translated to ordain, in Acts 14: 23, Dr. Robinson, in his Greek Lexicon, says, means "*to stretch*

[1] The New Englander, November, 1857, pp. 547–549.

out the hand, to hold up the hand, as in voting; hence *to vote, to give one's vote,* by holding up the hand. In the New Testament, *to choose by vote, to appoint.*" But in no case does the word mean *to ordain.* The only question, then, at issue with regard to the meaning of Acts 14 : 23 is, whether the apostles appointed the elders by a popular election, or by electing them themselves. The great preponderance of the best authorities is in favor of the opinion that the election was strictly popular. It is so understood by Calvin, Beza, Erasmus, Owen, Doddridge, Coleman, and many others. "This conclusion," says Dr. Lyman Coleman, "is sustained by the most approved authorities. According to Suicer, the primary and appropriate signification of the term is to denote *an election made by the uplifting of the hand,* and particularly denotes the election of a bishop by vote. 'In this sense,' he adds, 'it continued for a long time to be used in the church, denoting, not an *ordination* or *consecration,* but an election.' Grotius, Meyer, and De Wette so interpret the passage, to say nothing of Beza, Böhmer, Rothe, and others.

"To the same effect is also the following extract from Tindal. 'We read only of the apostles, constituting elders *by the suffrages of the people,* Acts 14: 23, which, as it is the genuine signification of the Greek word, χειροτονήσαντες, so it is accordingly interpreted by Erasmus, Beza, Diodati, and those who translated the Swiss, French, Italian, Belgic, and even English Bibles, till the Episcopal correction, which leaves out the words *by election,* as well as the marginal notes, which affirm that the apostles did not thrust pastors into the church through a lordly superiority, *but chose and placed them there by the voice of the congregation.*' Tyndale's translation is as follows: 'And when they had ordened them seniours by eleccion, in every congregacion, after they had preyde and fasted, they commennd them to God, on whom they beleved.' "[1]

A few modern biblical scholars, however, as, for instance, Professor H. B. Hackett and Dr. Samuel Davidson, maintain that nothing more can be *positively* learned from the passage in Acts 14: 23 than that the apostles themselves appointed the elders. Still, according to these authorities, there was undoubtedly a concurrent appointment. "One thing is clear to the candid inquirer," says Dr. Davidson, "that Paul and Barnabas appointed the elders in question." But in answer to the question, Did they make this appointment without the concurrence of the churches themselves? he replies: "We think not. The spirit of similar transactions, and the general tenor of the New Testament, forbid the supposition. Even in appointing an apostle, the company of the believers took a prominent part. The apostles did not complete their own number of themselves. The popular will was consulted. So, too, in the case of deacons. Hence it may be fairly inferred that the appointment of elders, here recorded, was not made contrary to the wish of the disciples. It is impossible to discover whether the people signified their wishes to Paul and Barnabas, by pointing out to them individuals whom they judged to be qualified for office; or whether the two did, in the first instance, constitute and set over the disciples Christians known to themselves, the people wisely concurring in the measure adopted for their edification by men divinely authorized to collect and organize Christian communities. In either case, the people's wishes were not contravened. Whether *the initiative act* originated with the members or the two apostles, we do not undertake to decide. One thing alone must be maintained, that all was done with the

[1] See Primitive Church, by Dr. Lyman Coleman, p. 63.

full approval of the brethren."[1] He afterwards affirms, that "there is even a probability that the disciples had chiefly to do with their election." Neander likewise says: "The brethren chose their own officers from among themselves; or if, in the first organization of the churches, their officers were appointed by the apostles, it was with the approbation of the members of the same."[2] This learned historian also repeatedly affirms that the apostles distinctly taught that the sovereignty under Christ was exclusively in the hands of the brotherhood of the local church. Consequently, whoever, in the first instance, made the nomination or appointment of a church officer, it must have been done subject to the final action of the church. The veto power was not with any church officer or judicatory, but with the brethren of the church.

NOTE C.

Undoubtedly, the purer Congregationalism, or the nearer it is kept to the primitive model of church government, the more efficient it will be in the maintenance and dissemination of a living Christianity. It is possible that our Congregationalism has lost something of its power by being burdened with a few things, which do not necessarily belong to it as a system. In this view it is not uninstructive to see how a foreign divine, who has bestowed much study upon the ecclesiastical polity of the New Testament, and is himself a Congregationalist, looks upon American Congregationalism. "In reference to councils and associations," says Dr. Samuel Davidson, "our opinion is, that, if it be deemed

[1] Ecclesiastical Polity of the New Testament, by Samuel Davidson, D. D., pp. 161, 162.

[2] Primitive Church, by Dr. Coleman, Introduction, p. 19.

desirable to have them at all, they should be sparingly summoned, and only in cases of great difficulty; that duties should not be assigned to them which can as well be managed otherwise; and that they should lay no restraint on the internal and inalienable liberties of the individual churches. We repeat our assertion, that they are too frequently called by the Congregationalists of New England; and that by practice, matters have come to be assigned them which need not and ought not to be so transferred. Thus they *license* men to preach the gospel; *ordain* those called to be pastors; deliberate on the removal of a minister from one place to another, and depose a pastor from his office. These and other things should not be consigned to councils or associations, because they may be transacted equally well by the churches themselves in their individual capacity, each of which is competent to manage its own affairs. The cases which justify the calling of a council should be doubtful and difficult, deeply affecting the purity of a church in doctrine and discipline, or the rights of parties belonging to it.

"As to *standing* councils or *consociations*, they are exposed to so many objections that they ought to be discarded. For their undoubted tendency is *to invite* or *encourage* cases of appeal, to foster elements of strife, and to prepare the way for abridgment of the liberties rightfully belonging to every Christian church. We object to them as injurious to the general interests of truth and freedom. We should not wish to see them erected. Far distant be the day when the consociations of Connecticut shall appear in the mother country among our Congregational churches! Unlike the stated associations formed among us in most counties, they end to Presbyterianism."[1]

[1] Ecclesiastical Polity of the New Testament, by Dr. S. Davidson. Second Edition, pp. 270, 271.

Again this author remarks: "We know that in cases of dispute between pastor and people, it is common among American Congregationalists to summon *mutual* or *ex parte* councils, to examine, hear evidence, and vote accordingly; but although their decision be obligatory on the parties no farther than the parties themselves consent, the propriety of the step is exceedingly questionable. To say the least, it is wholly unnecessary. A church has power, according to the general principles on which it is organized, to adjust and perform every act of discipline, whether it concerns pastors or members, as American Congregationalists themselves freely admit. To erect, therefore, any other tribunal for the occasion, is perfectly arbitrary and useless; virtually implying, on the part of those who summon it, a distrust in the sufficiency, or defect in the luminousness, of the comprehensive code by which all the affairs of Christian men must be ultimately determined. We disapprove of such councils. It is better to keep the institutions of Christ simple, as they appear in the New Testament. Better is it to allow a church the exercise of its own rights *fully*, without sanctioning so much as the appearance of incompleteness. The utility of the proceeding in question is not clear, while the superfluousness of it is apparent. Hence it should not be resorted to." [1]

It should be said in justification of our custom of licensing candidates for the ministry, that a *license* from an association is simply a *recommendation* of the candidate from so many ministers to the churches. They simply *advise* the churches to hear him preach. The license has no ecclesiastical authority whatever, and no force except what it derives from the character and influence of the men

[1] Ecclesiastical Polity of the New Testament, by Dr. Davidson. Second Edition, p. 320.

who gave it. With regard to the action of ordaining and dismissing, and mutual and *ex parte* councils, it is unquestionably true that they often assume authority which they do not possess. The style of language which they use in their *results* is often exceedingly objectionable. When called, for instance, *to advise* a church with regard to dismissing its minister, the council not unfrequently takes the business entirely into its own hands, and, after hearing a representation of the case, of its own authority *pronounces* the minister *dismissed.* "And hereby," they say, "*he is dismissed.*" Other assumptions of authority, equally glaring and equally inconsistent with the fundamental principles of Congregationalism, are frequently made by councils; and there are reasons of the most imperative nature why every practice of this kind should be at once corrected. The brethren of every local church should understand that the sovereignty under Christ, and all the responsibilities that attach to that sovereignty, are entirely with themselves; and also that the sovereignty of the local church is indivisible and incommunicable; that it cannot even be shared, without occasioning its destruction, with any officer or judicatory above the church. And an ecclesiastical council should always make the impression, both by their demeanor and their language, that their work is simply *advisory* or *persuasive,* or, as in the case of their actually ordaining a minister, that they act simply as *the servants of the church,* performing the work of its members for them, and only at their request. It should not only be understood, but it should be more distinctly and formally acknowledged than it usually is, both by the ordaining council and the members of the church, that the ordaining power is vested in the church, and not in the council. It would also frequently be a great gain to the disciplinary power of a church, often preventing cases of prolonged and troublesome discipline, if all the members, and especially the erring brother, distinctly understood that the final action of the church upon his case will be *decisive;* unless the church, in its own sovereignty, shall see fit to take the advice of other churches. This last course may sometimes show a spirit of candor, and a commendable desire to do justly; still it is the *right* of a church, after it has once passed a vote excommunicating an erring member, from that time forth to "*let him be* a heathen man and a publican," and that *letting him be* will often save a church from the most prolonged and disastrous difficulties.

The sovereignty of the local church is as essential to Congregationalism as to Independency, and any thing which is destructive of that principle of church polity is destructive of Congregationalism. The distinction between Independency and Congregationalism is not that Independency says that ecclesiastical councils *shall not* be employed, while Congregationalism says that they *shall* be employed, in certain cases; but it is rather this, that according to Independency ecclesiastical councils *ought not* to be employed, while according to Congregationalism they *may rightfully* be employed sometimes to advise or to assist, because such a use of them is not in the least degree destructive of the sovereignty of the local church; and, if they *may rightfully* be employed, it is *expedient* to employ them in certain cases, not only for the sake of the assistance thus obtained, but also because it is Christian courtesy, and tends to promote the good order and the fellowship of the churches. But to admit that ecclesiastical councils have power or authority to do any thing which a local church has no power or authority to do, is destructive of one of the essential principles of Congregationalism, the sovereignty of each church. To admit, for instance, that a local church has no power or right, without an ecclesiastical council, to ordain its own minister or to dismiss him even though both the church and the minister desire the separation and agree to it, is to admit that a council has an ecclesiastical authority higher than that of the local church. Such an admission is a surrender of Congregationalism. It breaks down at once the most important distinction between the church polity of the primitive Christians and the centralized and despotic forms of church government. If councils are absolutely necessary, it would be as well, nay better, to have *standing* councils or presbyteries; and if we should have presbyteries we should have synods, and so on. We must, at all hazards, maintain the sovereignty, under Christ, of the local church, and also its absolute completeness as an ecclesiastical body, or, in other words, its competency to transact all ecclesiastical business. A church *can*, according to the principles of *Congregationalism*, ordain its own minister; and this was the practice among the earlier Congregational churches of New England. A church *can*, according to the principles of *Congregationalism*, dismiss its minister upon mutual agreement between themselves and him, or without such agreement, if he is morally unworthy of his place. But while Congregationalism strenuously maintains this *right* of individual churches as absolutely necessary to their sovereignty, it is also Congregational and advisable, always, when it can be done, to ask for the advice of other churches, both in ordaining and in dismissing a minister.

We cannot refrain here from venturing the suggestion, that it would serve to keep more prominently in the minds of both the ministers and the members of our churches the great fact of the sovereignty of each local church, if it was the custom for the church asking advice always to take formal action upon the question submitted, *after* having received the advice of the council. Let the action of the church be consistent with the language of the letter missive. If that asks for advice, let the church meet and receive the advice, and take formal action upon it. And always, unless by the letter missive, or in some other way the church particularly directs otherwise, let the *final* action be the action of the church, and not of the council. The influence of such a practice would in various ways be healthful. It would forcibly remind both the council and the church of their relative positions. It would prevent many unintentional, and perhaps some intentional, violations of the first principles of Congregationalism.

NOTE D.

History furnishes numerous illustrations of the tendency of centralized systems of church government to become more and more centralized. Not only do these systems often give to individuals who are educated under their influence a craving for a still more despotic government, and so send them on in advance from one church to another, until they reach the church of absolute despotism; but these systems themselves we often see gradually changing and moving on in the same direction. Does a church organize itself partly after the Presbyterian and partly after the Congregational model, the tendency is not towards Congregationalism, but towards Presbyterianism. Is a Presbyterian church of the United States of America organized, discarding, under the influence of certain Congregational elements in it, some of the features of Presbyterianism, as for instance its denominational boards, the tendency is not towards a more perfect Independency, but towards a more intense Presbyterianism. One degree of centralization in church government begets another degree, and that still another, and so on; the change is seldom in the opposite direction, except under the influence of religious reformation.

"It is well known," says Dr. Coleman, "that the introduction of Episcopacy into this country gave rise to a long and bitter controversy. The objection, made from within the Episcopal churches as well as from without, was, that its form of government is anti-republican, and opposed to the spirit of our free institutions. The House of Burgesses in Virginia, composed chiefly of Episcopalians, declared their abhorrence of bishops, unless at the distance of three thousand miles, and denounced 'the plan of introducing them, in the most unexceptionable form, on this side of the Atlantic, as a pernicious project.'

"When, at last, Episcopacy was introduced, it was only by a compromise, — the Episcopalian churches consenting to submit to diocesan Episcopacy only in a form greatly modified, and divested of its most obnoxious features. To the exclusion of the laity from a free and full participation in the affairs of the government, they would not for a moment submit. Such, according to Bishop White, was the prejudice of Episcopalians, 'against the name, and much more against the office of a bishop, that, but for the introduction of the laity into the government of the church, no general organization would probably have been formed.' Accordingly, the people were allowed freely to choose their own pastors, and to have a full representation in all their courts. This American Episcopacy was so modified, and the prelatical powers of the bishop so restricted by the checks and balances of republican principles, that the English prelates, on the other hand, were reluctant to confer the Episcopate upon Bishop White, alleging that he 'entertained a design to set up Episcopacy on the ground of *presbyterial and lay authority.*'

"Such was American Episcopacy at first, — qualified as much as possible, by the infusion of popular principles, to restrain the arbitrary powers of the bishop. But what now has this same Episcopacy become? What now the powers of the bishop, compared with what they then were? He possesses power almost as arbitrary as that of an Eastern despot; and assumes to rule by an authority independent of the will of his subjects. The bishops are permanent and irresponsible monarchs, restrained by no judicial tribunal. The house of bishops admit no order of the inferior clergy to their general convention. They ordain, depose, and restore to the ministry at pleasure whom they will; 'so that a Puseyite bishop may fill the church with impenitent and unconverted men.' He can prevent any congregation from settling the minister of their choice, or displace one at his will, and may, '*upon probable cause*,' forbid any clergyman from another diocese to officiate in his own. Such is the fearful nature of those powers which are now intrusted to this spiritual despot in our free republic.

"And yet, as if all this ominous accumulation of Episcopal prerogatives were not enough, the claims of the bishops are still pressed higher and higher. The house of bishops, with all its powers, has been superinduced upon the general convention since its establishment in America. Now these privileged hierarchs can only be tried *by themselves*; that is, if a president be guilty of any crime or misdemeanor whatever, he must be impeached and tried by a jury of *presidents alone;* a governor by a jury of governors. In one convention, the bishop lately claimed and exercised the prerogative of adjusting the roll of the members, denying to them the right of all deliberative assemblies, — that of deciding upon the qualifications of their own members; and the same convention, 'by a vote of nearly three to one,' meekly acquiesced in this claim of their prelate. Another convention provides that its proceedings '*shall not be open to the public*.' It gives to the bishop an absolute veto upon all their acts; and, to crown the whole, makes him 'the judge in all ecclesiastical trials.'

. . . .

"Consider, now, this enormous extension of the Episcopal power in this enlightened age, in this free republic, — this monstrous spiritual despotism imposed upon a people jealous above all men of their rights, and prompt to repel every invasion of them; — contemplate such a people, under such circumstances, with scarcely a feeble note of remonstrance bowing themselves down to this hierarchal supremacy, and shall we wonder at the early rise of a mild and comparatively unformed Episcopacy? Shall we marvel at the gradual extension of its influence over feeble churches, dependent for their support and protection? Why should this be thought a thing incredible, in view of what is transpiring in the midst of us?"[1]

Such facts as these, of which the history of centralization in church government is full, are a loud warning to Congregationalists to maintain, at all costs and in all their integrity, the principles of their free and divine church polity; and never, under any circumstances, to compromise them with the first degree of centralization. It was by this process of gradually yielding up these principles, beginning with the slightest possible surrender of them, that the first churches, those left by the apostles and primitive Christians, lost their divine form and power, passing on from one degree of centralization and corruption to another, until finally they ended in all the abominations and the unparalleled despotism of Rome. A fearful responsibility is resting upon the Congregationalists of the present age, and especially upon those of this country. A world's interests are in the issue. And it is due to the great Author of their church polity, — it is due to all the coming ages of the world, that they be found faithful to their trust.

[1] Primitive Church, pp. 263–266.

NOTE E.

The more candid and intelligent Episcopalians even admit that the first Christian churches were, in government, entirely independent of each other; and that there were only two kinds of church officers, presbyters or ministers and deacons, there being no distinction between a presbyter and a bishop. Dr. Coleman cites the following Episcopalian authorities: "At first," says the learned Dr. Barrow, "every church was settled apart under its own bishop and presbyters, so as independently and separately to manage its own concerns. Each was governed by its own head, and had its own laws."[1] "The subordinate government," says Riddle, "of each particular church, was vested in itself; that is to say, the whole body elected its ministers and officers, and were consulted concerning all matters of importance. All churches were independent of each other, but were united by the bonds of holy charity, sympathy, and friendship."[2] "Though there was one Lord, one faith, one baptism," says Archbishop Whately, "yet they were each a distinct, independent community on earth, united by the common principles on which they were founded by their mutual agreement, affection, and respect; but not having any one recognized head on earth, or acknowledging any sovereignty of one of those societies over others. Each bishop originally presided over one entire church."[3] "Bingham, and Chancellor King, and multitudes of the most respectable writers in the communion of the Episcopal church," says Dr. Coleman, "fully sustain the foregoing representations of the right of suffrage, as enjoyed by the primitive churches. They are

[1] Coleman's Primitive Church, p. 50. [2] Ibid. p. 51.
[3] Ibid. p. 51.

clearly supported by the late Dr. Burton, and by Riddle, both of Oxford University, and by the best authorities, both ancient and modern. 'The mode of appointing bishops and presbyters,' says Riddle, 'has been repeatedly changed. Election by the people, for instance, has been discontinued. This is, indeed, in the estimation of Episcopalians, a great improvement; but still, as they must allow, it is a change."[1] "A volume," says Dr. Coleman, "might be filled with authorities from the English Church alone, in which both her most distinguished prelates and her most eminent scholars concede to presbyters a virtual equality with bishops, and the right to ordain."

"The Necessary Erudition of a Christian Man, drawn up with great care, approved by both houses of Parliament in 1543, and prefaced by an epistle from the king himself, declares that 'priests [presbyters] and bishops are, by God's law, one and the same; and that the powers of ordination and excommunication belong equally to both. . . . Archbishop Usher, one of the brightest ornaments of the Episcopal church, on being asked by Charles I., in the Isle of Wight, whether he found in antiquity that '*presbyters alone did ordain*,' answered, '*Yes*,' and that he would show his majesty more — 'even where *presbyters* alone successively ordained *bishops*.'"[2]

And yet there is reason to believe, that many in the Episcopal church, and not a few even of its clergy, tenaciously cherish the belief that theirs is the church of the apostolic age, and that out of it there is no valid ordination, and, of course, none who ought to be recognized as ministers of Christ. "Take any other church," they say, "and trace back its history, and you will find its origin somewhere this side of the age of the apostles; but not so with the Epis-

[1] Coleman's Primitive Church, p. 69. [2] Ibid. p. 193.

copal church, for that is of the same age with Christianity." But we have only to deliver over such persons with their too limited knowledge to the more intelligent members of their own communion. Riddle acknowledges that there has been a *change*, and claims that Episcopacy is a "*great improvement*" upon the church polity of the apostles! This is frank and honest. Presbyterianism and Methodism are likewise professedly improvements upon Episcopacy. Methodism had its origin with John Wesley, in the first half of the eighteenth century. Presbyterianism had its origin with John Calvin, about the middle of the sixteenth century. Modern Episcopacy had its origin only 'a few years earlier in the same century, with Henry VIII., who established it solely as a means of justifying his crime of divorcing the queen, and marrying one of the queen's maids of honor.' It is "a fragment broken off from the Papal despotism." Or, if Episcopacy be traced back through all the abominations of the Roman Catholic Church, it had its origin, according to the most accredited historians, sometime in the second century, in a slight distinction, then for the first time introduced, between a bishop and a presbyter. This new kind of a bishop was at first simply the presbyter who presided at the board of the presbyters of a single local church. He was the president of the presbytery of a single church. From this the rise of Episcopacy was very gradual, the bishop in subsequent centuries claiming more and more authority, and the people surrendering their rights one after another, until finally the Pope took the place of the already despotic bishop, and the government of the church, which at first was a pure democracy, became an absolute despotism.

With regard to the Episcopal doctrine of apostolic succession, in addition to what was said on pages 33, 34, the following remarks of Rev. Albert Barnes are exceedingly pertinent: "Nothing in history can be more hopeless than the effort to make out the actual spiritual descent of Bishop White or Hobart as prelatical bishops in a direct uncontaminated line, from the college of the apostles, or from any one of the apostles; and nothing that assumes to be a grave matter is more ridiculous or contemptible than the attempt, with a grave face, to exhibit such a demonstration. There is not a pecuniary claim of the smallest possible value, or a claim of any other kind, that could be defended on that ground before a court of quarter-sessions; — not a title to an heir-loom, or to a right of common, or to an acre of land, that could be maintained for a moment on such an argument, and no sensible man would for a moment regard *any* pretended right as of the slightest value, that did not rest on a better foundation. It is a most marvellous thing, that sensible men persist in asserting their belief in any such ascertainable pedigree, or in its worth, even if it could be ascertained. Where, in all the New Testament, is there the slightest hint, that the validity of the ministry depends on the fact of such an ascertained descent, or that a ministry is invalid where such a pedigree cannot be made out? If the New Testament *had* asserted this, the assertion would now strip all Episcopalians, as well as all others, of any right to administer the ordinances of religion, and at once degrade the whole of them to the condition of laymen."[1]

NOTE F.

Congregationalism is not a *monarchy*, like Popery; nor *prelacy*, like Episcopalianism; nor an *oligarchy*, like Presbyterianism; but is *democratic* or *republican* in government.

[1] See an article on Exclusivism, by Rev. Albert Barnes, in the Presbyterian Quarterly Review for March and June, 1857.

The friends of centralization in church government in this country are very fond of instituting comparisons between their several systems and the form of our civil government. They thus seek to commend their several church organizations to the favorable regard of a liberty-loving people. But, to say nothing of Papacy, when Episcopacy institutes such a comparison in favor of itself, the most remarkable thing about it is the boldness with which it presumes upon the ignorance and the credulity of those whom it hopes to influence. Episcopacy, even in this country, is a spiritual despotism. The laity are only mocked with a shadow of power. In the election of a minister, if the choice of the parish is agreeable to the bishop, very well; but if not, there is no way for the parish to obtain the minister of its own choice. The election by the parish amounts to a mere *nomination* to the bishop. The sole *privilege* of the people is to give *information.* They are entirely dependent upon the will of the bishop for both the valid election and ordination of their minister. And so of the lay deputies in the Episcopal conventions; so long as they deliberate and vote agreeably to the will of the bishops and the clergy, they may think themselves of some importance; but in opposition to that will they can do nothing — absolutely nothing. Thus the clergy are really elected by the bishop. And who elects the bishop? The clergy of a diocesan convention choose him, and then *nominate* him to the lay deputies. And to whom is the bishop accountable? To the power that elects him? By no means. To the people? Not at all; but only to his fellow bishops. Thus every thing is in the hands of the bishops. In the general convention they alone constitute the upper house, and possess "the exclusive right to propose acts for the concurrence of the other house," which is composed of clerical and lay delegates. Now what possible similarity has this government to that of our republic? When the chief magistrates of the several states shall be chosen for life, and shall be accountable only to a board of their own number; when no town officers can be chosen except at the option of the official head of the state; when these chief magistrates are themselves chosen by the town officers; when the people have no power, of their own sovereign will, either to place over themselves their own officers or to depose them; when, in short, the sovereignty in these United States is no longer with the people, but exclusively in the hands of their officers, then, and then only, may Episcopacy begin to claim our favorable regard on the ground of its marked resemblance to our civil government.

The following remarks, with regard to Episcopacy in this country, are too true. "Every thing is in the hands of the bishops, who are farthest removed from the laity, and have least sympathy with them. The bishops are absolute masters of the church. If they held their appointment from the laity, and represented their opinions and feelings, and if they held their appointment only for a term of years, the case would be different. But the bishops are not, in theory or in fact, the representatives of the laity, but their spiritual lords and masters."[1]

Nor can Methodism, any more than Episcopacy, claim the advantage of a resemblance to our civil government. Methodism, like Episcopacy and Papacy, is a spiritual despotism. It takes the sovereign power from the many, and gives it to the few. Its founder, John Wesley, himself declared, "*We are no republicans.*" "*As long as I live, the people shall have no share in choosing either stewards or leaders among the Methodists.*" "Certainly that system," it has been forcibly said, "which does not leave even their

[1] Organic Christianity, by L. A. Sawyer, p. 217.

houses of worship in the hands of the people who erected them, — which gives the people no vote in the choice of their religious teachers, — which leaves no question of discipline, — *no* important question, — to be finally decided by the people, *or even by those in whose appointment the people have had any agency,* — certainly such a system does not recommend itself to us by its republicanism."[1]

The Presbyterians, likewise, are especially fond of claiming that their church polity is eminently republican. It is, they say, like our republic, a strictly representative government. They affirm that there is a striking resemblance between its series of judicatories, on the one hand, and our state and national governments, and especially our judiciary system, on the other. But this comparison is fallacious. The true character of a government is determined not so much by the nature of its series of judicatories, as by the *relation* of that series to *the people,* — not so much by the internal working of the superstructure as by the nature of the *contact* of that superstructure with those governed. Does the government, whatever it is in its officers and its courts, have its origin immediately from the people; and is it constantly, or, at least, at regular and comparatively brief intervals, held accountable to the people for its conduct? or does it have its origin immediately from an oligarchy installed for life over the people? or does it originate from neither? These questions are decisive of the nature of a government. A government is despotic in its nature just in proportion as it is out of the hands of *the people;* and it is democratic or republican just in proportion as it is in their hands. We must scrutinize Presbyterianism, then, in its relation to the *local churches,* in order to understand its true nature as a system of government; and it is at just that decisive point.

[1] Congregational Tracts, No. 1, p. 14.

that its similarity to republicanism entirely fails. In Presbyterianism, the session is the church. When our town officers shall be chosen for life, and shall hold in their hands all the legislative and judicial and executive government of the town, subject only to the supervision of certain higher judicatories composed of representatives chosen not by the towns, but by their several boards of officers; when, in short, our town officers shall become themselves the town, and from them shall rise all the rest of the governmental machinery, then, and then only, may Presbyterianism begin to claim the favorable regard of the people on the ground of its striking resemblance to their civil government. "Presbyterianism," says David Hale, "is not republicanism, nor is it in any proper sense a representative government. If the government of this nation had been organized by the election of a president and senate for life, in whom were vested all the powers of the constitution, what would it have been called? Not a representative government, certainly, nor a republic in any sense. It could have been called nothing but an *elective aristocracy*." The constitution and powers of the church session are such of themselves as to make this form of church government a perfect oligarchy. "Presbyterianism," says a recent writer, "is sometimes described and advocated by its friends as a system of church republicanism. The elders are considered as representatives of the churches, and the churches are considered as administering their affairs, in all the church courts, on the representative principle. But this is an entire mistake. There is no representation of the church in the church courts. All those courts are established over the church, and are independent of it. . . .

"The session is not a representative court, in which the elders represent the church. To make it such, the eldership ought to be appointed annually, or for a term of years.

It is rather a court of monarchs, or aristarchs, who hold their office for life ; a limited monarchy, indeed, as so called monarchies in the state usually are ; but a real monarchy, nevertheless ; or, more strictly, an aristarchy of rulers appointed for life, and ruling on the principle of elective aristarchy. . . . .

"The half representation, which, in effect, is somewhat less than half, often not a fourth, in presbyteries and synods, is a representation of the eldership, the aristarchy of the churches, not the churches themselves. This is very far indeed from being republican representation of the membership.

"General assemblies are representative courts based on the presbyteries, in which the ministers and elders of the presbyteries are represented equally. The representation, therefore, is of essentially the same kind as that of the presbyteries.

"The ministers and elders of the Presbyterian church are accountable to presbyteries, subject to an appeal to the higher courts, but are not accountable to the membership. The government of the Presbyterian churches, therefore, is as much a despotism as that of the Methodists, the Episcopalians, and the Roman Catholics.

"It was designed to be an improved system of Episcopacy, restricting the bishop to a parish, and the presbyters to the exercise of parish jurisdiction, and governing the larger districts of the church by courts of bishops, assisted by equal numbers of presbyters. The principles of the Presbyterial and Episcopal systems are the same. Neither allows the powers of church government to be vested in the membership; neither gives the membership any controlling influence in determining the form and organization of the church, or directing its policy and discipline." [1]

[1] Organic Christianity, by L. A. Sawyer, pp. 247–8–9.

"The objections to it are the same as to all other modifications of Episcopacy, and all other despotisms. It is not scriptural, it is not the original, divinely appointed plan of church organization, which was purely democratic; and, secondly, it is not expedient. The democratic plan is safer and better. This appears from a critical examination of the New Testament on the subject; and it is still further illustrated by the history and fruits of Presbyterianism, and its condition and tendencies at the present time."[1]

With regard to the natural political affinities of different denominations, history abundantly teaches that the more centralized the system of church government which men advocate, the more despotic the civil government which they prefer. It is a notorious historical fact, that in the time of the American Revolution, where the Congregational church polity prevailed there was the greatest enthusiasm among the people in the Declaration of Independence, and in the formation of a republican government; and where other systems of church polity prevailed, there was the least enthusiasm. The Episcopalians, as a class, were tories. They were determined to continue their allegiance to the British crown. The Presbyterians, as a class, were far more indifferent to the result than the Congregationalists. The Congregationalists, as a class, were fully resolved to be satisfied with nothing less than a strictly independent and republican government.

The political affinities of these several denominations have also been clearly developed in the history of England. Episcopacy has always been, in that country, the persistent friend and supporter of monarchy, and the natural enemy of religious toleration and civil liberty. Hence it came to be a motto with the tyrannical James, "no bishop, no king." "The friends of liberty," says Dr. Robert Vaughan, speak-

[1] Organic Christianity, by L. A. Sawyer, pp. 251, 252.

ing of the Anglican Church, "have always had to lay their account with her opposition, when endeavoring to expand the principles of freedom. Her concessions in this way have always come late, reluctantly, and with a bad grace." Macaulay likewise says, that the Church of England, from the time of its establishment, "continued to be, for more than one hundred and fifty years, the servile handmaid of monarchy and the steady enemy of public liberty."

The Presbyterians, while their church polity is a great improvement upon Papacy and Episcopacy, and while they have done much in weakening the power of despotism, yet never have been such bold and uncompromising advocates of human freedom and republican government as have the Congregationalists. It is a well-known fact, that at the time of the Westminster Assembly, the Presbyterians were generally royalists and bigotedly conservative, while the Independents were thorough republicans, and wished for an entire reconstruction of the government after the republican model. "The relations of Presbyterianism and Independency in England, during the period of the civil war and the ascendency of Cromwell, are remarkable. But for Independency, Presbyterianism would have subverted the religious liberties of England in favor of an exclusive Presbyterian national church establishment. But for Presbyterianism, Independency would have succeeded in obtaining permanent toleration for herself, and for other Protestant denominations."[1] It is a very significant historical fact, that Presbyterianism in England "fell in consequence of its own active exertions to cast down its Congregationalist competitors, and to exalt itself at their expense." Yet it is but the natural fruit of this church polity, that its adherents were unwilling to tolerate Congre-

[1] Organic Christianity, by L. A. Sawyer, pp. 379–380.

gationalism, and that they united as they did with the Episcopalians in a carefully laid plot to crush it. But they were caught in their own snare, and overwhelmed. The monarch whom they raised to the throne made them the first victims of his despotism. We will be thankful for all the good which holy men in the Presbyterian church have done. But their system of church government is exposed to all the objections of every despotic ecclesiastical organization. It is unscriptural; and is particularly unsuitable to educate a republican people to appreciate and maintain their civil freedom. An oligarchical government in the church cannot promote republicanism in the state.

NOTE G.

The advocates of centralized systems of church government, particularly Episcopalians and Presbyterians, are very fond of claiming that theirs are the *conservative* churches. Great stress is laid upon this claim, and it is very effective in its influence with great numbers of well-meaning people. But the good word *conservative*, in this case, is made to play a very deceptive part, for such have come to be the associations of the term, that people forget, that what is evil may be conserved as well as what is good, and therefore are not careful to inquire for the *particular things* of which these church organizations claim to be conservative. Should this inquiry be made, it will generally be found that the claimants prefer to stop with the word conservative, and make no specifications. The hoops of a cask will hold the most vile and fetid wine as securely as the most pure and sparkling; but it would not be particularly sensible nor honest for a seller of the wine to be continually ringing changes upon the strength of the hoops, and at the same time decline to speak of what is within. These centralized church organizations assume to be far more conservative than Congregationalism. But more conservative of what, we ask? We have a right to the specifications. More conservative of civil and religious liberty? If so, it is something worth mentioning. But where is the man of ordinary intelligence who ever thought of making a comparison, in this particular, in favor of church centralization? More conservative, then, of popular education, and of the general intelligence of the people? Facts and statistics, now known and read of all men, would at once unmask the presumption of such a claim, if any one should be bold enough to make it. More conservative, is it said, then, of the general thrift and enterprise, of the material prosperity, of the masses of the people? Let New England, in this regard, be compared with any or all of those portions of the world where other systems of church government prevail, and would any advocate of church centralization wish to publish the result? More conservative, then, of true piety, of that "mind which was in Christ Jesus"? It would become us to reply to this charge with great humility. And yet it is proper to test Congregationalism in this respect by the rule of the Saviour, "Ye shall know them by their fruits." Let, then, the religious character of the Pilgrims, and of those generally who have adopted their church polity, answer; let the history of revivals in New England, let the standard of piety in the New England churches, their efficiency in the service of Christ, the missionary spirit that pervades them, the amount of their Christian benevolence, — let these fruits, and such as these, answer. But in respect to all these particulars now mentioned, vital and all important as they are, no advocate of a centralized church government ever dares to draw any comparison between Congregationalism and his own system. For it is too prominently written on the page of history ever to be denied, that it was Congregationalism standing side by side with Presbyterianism and Episcopacy, and in spite of their combined resistance, that saved English liberty at its last gasp, and also that it was this same church polity that gave birth to American republicanism. It is likewise too well known ever to be denied, that under no other form of church government has so much been done, and so successfully, for popular education and for the moral elevation of the masses of the people. And in respect to the last most important particular, a living and effective piety, while we humble ourselves before God, we say, let the world judge of the different church polities by their fruits. An eminent Episcopal writer admits, that "the most ultra churchman says nothing against the personal piety of [his] Protestant brethren." And certainly the Presbyterians will not be very forward to draw any comparison in this respect in their favor, when, in large branches of their church, no evidence of regeneration is necessary for admission to the church; but, on the contrary, all except the "ignorant" and the "scandalous" are cordially received.[1]

More conservative, then, we ask again, of what? Of evangelical truth; of "the faith once delivered to the saints"? This is frequently asserted; but we have looked in vain for any thing that could be called even a proximate proof of the truth of such an assertion. Both Episcopalians and Presbyterians often point ominously to Massachusetts, and each affirm, that, had their church polity prevailed here, the Unitarian apostasy never would have occurred. This is a standing affirmation; it has been made again and again in private conversation and in the public prints. A distinguished American bishop made it a few years since on a public occasion in London. But the Epis-

[1] See The Great Awakening, by Joseph Tracy, p. 22–24.

copalians forget that the first church that became Unitarian in this country was an Episcopalian church;[1] and the Presbyterians forget that the church over which the celebrated Dr. W. E. Channing was settled was once a Presbyterian church,[2] the oldest but one of their order in New England. The advocates of Episcopacy especially are very injudicious in thrusting their church into such a comparison. They are too fearfully exposed not to be terribly riddled themselves in turn, if they first cast that stone. It is already indelibly written of English Episcopacy on the page of history, that she has "a Popish ritual, a Calvinistic creed, and an Arminian clergy." Only "two thousand out of her twelve thousand ministers," it is said, can be called evangelical. "By far the largest portion of Episcopal ministers and members of the Episcopal Church everywhere," says Rev. Albert Barnes, "are decided Aminians in doctrine; and wherever Episcopacy propagates itself, it propagates, as a matter of course, the doctrines of Arminius." Again he says: "It would not be possible to make the whole Episcopal Church conform in doctrine to the obvious meaning of the Thirty-nine Articles, and still retain the Episcopal form of government."[3] Is it not true that the Episcopalian churches of Connecticut are to a great extent Arminian in doctrine? Is it not generally understood, that Episcopacy in that State is a very good substitute for Unitarianism? And yet we never hear of the Arminian apostasy in the Episcopal Church of Connecticut! This is accounted for, in part, by the fact, that practically such a centralized church has no power, without the aid of the State, to discipline its members to any great extent for doctrinal errors, without destroying itself. The Episcopalians of Connecticut could not, by

[1] King's Chapel, Boston.

[2] Federal Street Church, Boston.

[3] See article on Exclusivism in Presbyterian Quarterly Review for March and June, 1857.

any course of discipline, purge themselves of Arminianism, without causing the ruin of the entire fabric of their church. When error has thus obtained a foothold in a consolidated church, it is impossible for that church to conform to the apostolic rule, "*first* pure, *then* peaceable;" it can be peaceable only as it connives at and conceals its impurity. On account of the gradual and unobstructed course of error in such churches, but little commotion is made; and this, to an alarming extent, is the real conservatism of church centralization. It is the conservation of peace at the expense of purity. It is such conservatism as Luther had to contend with, and such as has always been one of the greatest foes to all real reformation and spiritual advancement. It is the conservatism of a church that needs above all things, and at any expense of commotion or revolution, the most radical reformation. It is the obvious teaching of ecclesiastical history, that centralization in church government is far less strenuous in its opposition to the insidious advances of sin and error than it is in its opposition to true reform. "It seems to be admitted," says Dr. Coleman, "by members of their own communion, that there is no discipline in the Episcopal Church." One of the English Episcopalian writers, whom he cites in proof of this statement, affirms, "I believe such a thing as any single presentation for notoriously immoral conduct has scarcely been heard of for a century." "A well-known clergyman of our own country, in assigning his 'reasons for preferring Episcopacy,' speaks of it as 'universally felt and admitted' that 'in no Christian denomination of the country is there so great a diversity of opinion [as in the Episcopal Church] about doctrine, church polity, etc. But we hear,' he adds, 'of no discipline on account of this diversity. The probability is, that discipline on these accounts would rend and break up the church.' And again he says: 'There is no church in the world that has in fact so great a diversity of opinion in her own bosom, as the Church of England, and not a little of downright infidelity.'"[1] And this, recollect, is the language of one who is giving his "Reasons for preferring Episcopacy." One reason is, that he will not be disciplined in that church for any opinions he may chance to cherish; no, not even if he becomes an infidel. Under this neglect of discipline for opinion, the Church of England, he thinks, "will recover the primitive vitality of Christianity, so as to have it pervading and animating her whole communion." "Nor is it less certain," he adds, "that by attempting discipline for opinions, she would forever blight all these prospects." And yet this is the church which boasts of being more conservative of "the faith once delivered to the saints" than is Congregationalism, and which claims that it would have saved New England from Unitarianism!

Is it not, moreover, a well-known fact, that the more rigorous discipline of other denominations has sent multitudes, whose Christian characters were such that they felt themselves in danger from that discipline, into the Episcopal Church for safety? Is it not true, that in New England the temperance reformation, and the strong protest of the Congregational churches against the sin of human oppression, have sent numbers into the bosom of Episcopacy to find quiet and peace! Well may Dr. Coleman significantly ask: "Why do the malecontents of other denominations, men of equivocal character if not of tarnished reputation, take refuge in such numbers in that church?" And yet this is the church polity whose advocates proclaim in high places that it would have saved Massachusetts from the Unitarian apostasy!

And then, again, how dare the Presbyterians continually ring changes, as they do, upon this same Unitarian defec-

[1] See Primitive Church, by Dr. L. Coleman, pp. 121, 122.

tion, to the disparagement of Congregationalism, and in favor of their own church polity? Is their ecclesiastical system so immaculate, as far as the sin of heresy is concerned, that they can afford to exult in this regard over the church polity of the Pilgrims?

There were in Massachusetts in 1854, fifteen hundred and twenty-one churches. Of these about one third were Trinitarian Congregational churches, while only one hundred and seventy-two were Unitarian. Nearly all the Unitarianism of New England, and indeed of this country, is confined to the State of Massachusetts, so that a comparison of the whole number of the churches of this order in the land, some two hundred and fifty, with the whole number of Trinitarian Congregational churches, probably nearly three thousand, renders this Unitarian defection still more inconsiderable.

Now, first, we ask, Is there no parallel to this in the history of Presbyterianism? Has Presbyterianism saved the Presbyterian Church of Switzerland from Arianism and Unitarianism? Good authority affirms that the church of the land of Calvin "has greatly declined from its adherence to the Calvinistic doctrines, and has not only gone over to Arianism, but has gone far beyond, to Unitarianism and humanitarianism." Has the Presbyterianism of England saved the churches of this order there from a similar apostasy? It is a well-known fact, that nearly all the English Presbyterian churches are Unitarian. Has the Presbyterianism of this country been proof against all heresy? Is there no Arminianism among the Old School Presbyterians? A distinguished divine and scholar of New England, a man not given to fault-finding, still less to heresy-hunting, the late Professor B. B. Edwards, while on a tour at the South, wrote, "I have heard more Arminianism since I have been here than I ever heard before in my life." And then how is it with the Cumberland Presbyterians? Did their church government save them from becoming professedly Arminian? In 1837, did Presbyterianism save the Presbyterian Church of the United States from the so-called heresies of New Schoolism? Did it prevent the so-called apostasy of nearly one half of the churches of that communion? It does not seem that Presbyterianism has any great reason to exult so much over the fact, that out of the fifteen hundred and twenty-one churches of the State of Massachusetts, one hundred and seventy-two are Unitarian.

But, secondly, we affirm that there is abundant reason to warrant the belief, that, had all the churches of Massachusetts been bound together by some one of the consolidating systems of church government, the whole body would have sunk irrecoverably into Unitarianism. Not even a remnant of the churches could have disentangled themselves from the falling mass, and maintained in its integrity the faith of the Pilgrims. For when a doctrinal error has once obtained a lodgement in a consolidated church, — and history shows that this is as easily accomplished in such a church as in any other, — one of two things more usually happens, either the church is rent in twain, or the whole body lapses into the error; and in either result the system of church government proves worse than nothing as a protection against heresy, for in both cases it serves greatly to extend and perpetuate the evil of the error. Not even the Church of Scotland has been able to maintain its integrity, and at the same time protect itself against so-called erroneous opinions; but in the violent discussion of certain constitutional questions, — questions of church and state, — questions, too, involving more or less the doctrine of the church, it has been broken into fragments; and hence we have what Rev. Albert Barnes so appropriately calls the "asteroidal fragments of the Scotch Church." On the other hand, in the English Church, sunk as it is into Arminianism and irreligion, we have an example of an entire body of consolidated churches lapsing, in spite of their creed, quietly and irrecoverably into religious error. We also have an example similar to this last in the case of the Old School Presbyterians in our own country, where the whole body of connected churches, in spite of their recorded professions, and in the face of the outraged moral sentiment and the earnest protestations of the Christian world, have virtually and practically committed themselves to the defence of American slavery. It would not be possible for the English Episcopal Church to bring the real doctrinal faith of the mass of its members up to their written creed, without a revolution that would prove the utter destruction of their church establishment. Nor would it be possible to bring the real faith of the Old School Presbyterian Church of this country up to their written creed upon the subject of slavery, without bringing on the dismemberment and utter ruin of that church. In no other way does a centralized system of church government exhibit so much power as in preventing reformation in the church, when once it has fallen into sin or error. Could Luther, with all the power of the Reformation, reform the Catholic Church? Could the Puritans reform the English Church? No more can the older branch of the Presbyterian Church in this country be reformed, when once it shall have fully prostituted itself to the defence of the divine right of American slavery. And thus, too, the Evangelical Churches of Massachusetts would have been irretrievably lost in the Unitarian apostasy had they all been helplessly bound together by some consolidating system of church government. Instead of the elastic and comparatively easy bound, with which evangelical religion, under the Congregational system, regained its position, it would have been held down by all the concentrated power of a great provincial or national ecclesiastical organization, and its return to its former position would have been rendered impossible except by a most violent and disastrous revolution, such probably as could never have been successfully carried through. But as it was, at the commencement of the Unitarian controversy in 1810, there were, in all, three hundred and sixty-one Congregational churches, and at the close of the controversy, or rather the more belligerent form of it, in 1840, there were four hundred and nine orthodox Congregational churches.

Where, then, is the evidence that these centralized systems of church government are more conservative of evangelical truth than is Congregationalism? It cannot be found either in the nature of these systems or in their history. On the contrary, the great mass of evidence, drawn from all sources upon this point, is most decidedly against them. "It is notorious, that when false doctrine has inundated the church, it has flowed in from the clergy, and not from the people; and when the people have been trusted with power commensurate with their spiritual culture, they have stimulated their pastors to a maintenance of the simple truth. Our ecclesiastical system educates the people *for* their responsibilities and *by* their responsibilities; it honors them in *training* them, and in the *purpose* for which they are trained. It thus gives them a conservative influence, and prompts the clergy to respect that influence. Accordingly, we find that an immense majority of the churches standing on the republican platform have retained the evangelical faith; while the larger part of those which have been ruled by a hierarchy have lapsed into error. A small faction of the Church of England, with its Calvinistic creed and its skilful apparatus for enforcing it, is designated by the epithet Evangelical; while the Congregationalists of England, with all their aversion to œcumenical symbols, are a model of unity in the evangelical belief. If the pastors were to abandon their faith, the people would stand fast upon it. It has been often objected, that among the fifteen hundred and twenty-one churches in the State of Massachusetts, one hundred and seventy-two are Unitarian. Still, Unitarianism has not flourished so vigorously in this Puritan Commonwealth as Deism has flourished under a more concentrated church government; not so extensively as, in the opinion of wise observers, it would have prevailed under any other than our free polity; for if the churches of Massachusetts had been amalgamated into one state confederation, it is supposed that nearly all of them would have gone where the few dominant spirits had led the way; and the Congregationalism of that venerable Commonwealth would probably have been — what the Presbyterianism of England now is — penetrated with Socinianism. The gracefulness of Buckminster, the amenity of Greenwood, the sober sense of Ware, the wit of Kirkland, the genius of Channing, the strength of Theophilus Parsons, himself a host, the fame of the University, the princely fortunes of the metropolis, would have carried the churches headlong, unless every church had been trained to stand on its own foothold, and feel its responsibility to God, rather than to the dignitaries of the state. The life of the churches in Massachusetts after the eruption of Unitarianism, when contrasted with the death-like torpor of the Prussian churches after the eruption of rationalism, affords an indisputable argument for the policy which trusts the conservation of the truth to a free people. It is a noteworthy fact, that those churches of New England whose Congregationalism was the most unshackled, remained the firmest against the Unitarian onset. While ecclesiastics who had a centralized government were oscillating or yielding, the Baptists, who stretched Congregationalism into Independency, stood erect in the faith. The late Professor Edwards, a divine eminent alike for his candor and accuracy, remarked, at the close of an extensive tour: 'Throughout all my travels in Europe, and in the Southern States of our own country, I have never heard the doctrines of total depravity, regeneration, atonement, sovereignty, decrees, and eternal punishment proclaimed in so pungent and uncompromising a style as I have ordinarily heard them among the Congregationalists of our North-Eastern States.'"[1]

Of what, then, are these centralized systems of church government more conservative than is Congregationalism? It is certainly true, that they are less conservative of evangelical truth, a living piety, and the active benevolence and general efficiency of Christians. If, now, there are any minor things worthy to be mentioned, of which they are more conservative, it belongs to those who affirm it to make the specifications and prove their assertion. We know of no proper end or influence of a church which is not best attained and conserved by the church polity of the Pilgrims and the primitive Christians. Let the people thoroughly inform themselves upon this subject, and be no longer deceived by an artful use of the popular term *conservative.* It is the true conservatism of Congregationalists to maintain in all its integrity the church polity of the apostles and first Christians. "The true conservatism of New England is to keep a fast hold of those principles which are inwrought into the very warp and woof of our political system; and where is radicalism, if not in attempting to eradicate the ecclesiastical polity which, for more than two hundred years, has been growing with our growth, and intertwining itself with the character of our people? Where is the disorganizing spirit and the far-famed sin of schism, if not in attempting to extirpate the usages of our Pilgrim fathers, men who were as well qualified by nature, as well fitted by intellectual and moral discipline, to lay the foundations of an apostolical church, as uninspired men ever were, or perhaps can be expected ever to be? The citizens of some States follow in the footsteps of their fathers from the mere

[1] Address before the American Congregational Union, by Prof. E. A. Park, D. D., pp. 38-40.

influence of veneration for the past. We should gather around the religious institutions of our Puritan ancestry, because they are in the spirit of the New Testament; because they are the most venerable of all our institutions; because they are homogeneous with our national character; because, when they fall, one prop of our civil liberties will fall with them."[1]

We close this Appendix with the remark, that while we have thus frankly expressed our convictions upon the subject of church polity, we are not insensible to the distinction between the essence of Christianity and any external form in which it may be conserved and propagated. True piety, in this world, is often cherished under the greatest external disadvantages; and, therefore, not unfrequently, especially in isolated cases, it is found flourishing under a most unfavorable church polity. According to the example and spirit of the Saviour, we are to love all our fellow men as endowed with immortal being, and capable of immortal happiness; but we cannot do this unless at the same time, and with an equal intensity, we hate their sins. It is the fine remark of Olshausen, that "the blaze of God's wrath is only one side of the flame of his love." We are to hate sin even if we should find it in an angel, and all the more because it is in an angel. So, on a similar principle, we extend the hand of cordial Christian fellowship to all who truly love our Lord and Saviour, Jesus Christ, and who hope for salvation only by faith in him as their Almighty Redeemer; and at the same time we most strenuously protest against any unscriptural church polity which any of these brethren in Christ may have adopted.

[1] Sermon on the Duties of the New England Clergy, by Prof. E. A. Park, D. D., pp. 16, 17.

www.ingramcontent.com/pod-product-compliance
Lightning Source LLC
LaVergne TN
LVHW021412110826
845150LV00007B/1890

* 9 7 8 1 4 2 5 5 1 1 0 2 9 *